TOOLS OF POWER

KURT ANDERSEN
MARK O'DONNELL
ROGER PARLOFF

# of Tools Power

THE
ELITIST'S
GUIDE
TO THE
RUTHLESS
EXPLOITATION
OF
EVERYBODY
AND
EVERYTHING

The Viking Press   New York

First published in 1980 by The Viking Press
625 Madison Avenue, New York, N.Y. 10022

Published simultaneously in Canada by
Penguin Books Canada Limited

LIBRARY OF CONGRESS CATALOGING IN PUBLICATION DATA
Andersen, Kurt.
Tools of power.
1. Success—Anecdotes, facetiae, satire, etc.
I. O'Donnell, Mark, joint author.   II. Parloff, Roger,
joint author.   III. Title.
HF5386.A573   650.1'0207   80-5511
ISBN 0-670-72039-9

Printed in the United States of America
Set in Times Roman

CONTENTS

A U T H O R S '
I N T R O D U C T I O N

Reader, us. Us, reader.

Now that that's out of the way, you're probably wondering what has compelled you to read this deceptively small-looking book. That, of course, is a tribute to our knowledge of *exploiting power,* including that of the press. Through a process we call *didactic osmosis,* you too can be upwardly mobilized for the sirloin gates of Success, and in less time than it took you to learn to forge your father's signature.

Our techniques have worked for thousands. Six years ago, we opened our nationwide chain of Success Clinics, modeled on our previous success operating the well-known Grub 'n' Grog franchise restaurants. Both enterprises involved shepherding groups of hungry-eyed executives to Formica tables and convincing them later that they had been nourished.

Why did we decide to write a *book* based on our proven system? After all, you can't walk into a book on Saturday morning and spend all day there watching restful filmstrips and drinking Sanka out of Styrofoam cups. Our motives may sound simple to you, and well they should: *We just want everyone in America to be a bigger success than everyone else.*

The authors are three noted experts in the field—a businessman, a psychologist, and a businessman-psychologist liaison, respectively. Working together, we have been likened to a well-oiled machine (yet no warranty for maintenance is implied or intended). For our research data, we interviewed and tested nearly every up-and-coming and up-and-went big businessperson in America. If we did not contact you, that should serve as proof enough that you need this book badly. We also performed controlled scientific tests at the well-equipped National Avarice Labs in Washington, D.C. There we observed the reaction of white mice to other white mice sitting at large desks, to white mice in blue suits versus brown suits, to white mice with little books versus white mice without little books, and so on. (The cheese bill alone would make your company's comptroller whistle.) Then everything was fed into a computer.

What will this book do for you? It will provide specific, obsessive, and arbitrary techniques for upgrading your dress, manner, speech, behavior, being, and ancestry. It will afford you a smugly privileged perspective on less self-aware businesspeople who've not read it themselves. And, incidentally, it will permit you—indeed, is already permitting you—to take an active, go-getter part in our great free enterprise system by having actually purchased a book published by a business.

Good luck!—though you won't be needing it, and it doesn't really exist, anyway, and neither do you.

Kurt Andersen
Mark O'Donnell
Roger Parloff

TOOLS OF POWER

SUCCESS

CAN BE YOURS, BUT FIRST, *YOU* MUST BE *ITS*

Would you persuade, speak of interest, not reason.
—Ben Franklin

That you've bought this volume is fair indication that you're in less than tip-top shape, powerwise. People who pore over sex manuals can be assumed to be searching out ways to expand or initiate their sensual joy. Likewise, an interested reader of the present work is by all odds closer in deportment to Lee Harvey Oswald than Giscard d'Estaing. You need help, and we're here to provide it. But first, before you begin your meteoric ascent, just how bad off are you?

Do you possess the animal magnetism required to stand up and be promoted? Is your sense of self-evolution powerful enough to put you on the hind-leg footing of the Stance for Success? (More on that later.)

Let's measure your Power Quotient with a simple test designed by a committee of respected pedants, and used with astonishing success by several high school guidance counselors and by the personnel department of at least one well-regarded success clinic.

Do you really want power? Will you know how to use it once you get it? And on whom?

I

Complete the following sentences.

1. The best things in life are _____.
   a. expensive but tasteful
   b. made from petroleum derivatives
   c. unavailable to me
   d. disappointing

2. Tomorrow is another _____.
   a. word for nothin' left to lose
   b. lunch date
   c. way of saying "the day following today"
   d. mockery of my every hope

3. If I found out my wife was having an affair with my boss, I'd _____.
   a. tell him what she likes
   b. tell her what he likes
   c. ask her to find out what my chances of promotion were
   d. speak to his wife and open the bidding at $10,000

4. All work and no play makes Jack _____.
   a. fondly remembered by his heirs
   b. able to afford costly ulcer treatments
   c. self-righteous
   d. a strictly imaginary employee

5. College doesn't teach you the answers, it ____ .
   a. makes you so insufferable no one can bear to ask you the questions
   b. raffles them off
   c. teaches you to answer questions with other questions
   d. takes a mature Italian woman to do that

6. The one thing I always put before business is ____ .
   a. a human sacrifice
   b. the application of deodorant
   c. for the record, my loved ones
   d. yet to come along

7. You have to spend money to make ____ .
   a. money
   b. certain kinds of noise
   c. sure certain photographs are kept from the newspapers
   d. yourself feel taller

8. It's not *what* you know, it's ____ .
   a. what *you* know
   b. what you *know*
   c. what you know far too well
   d. who or whom, I'm never sure which

9. If you want it done right, do it ____ .
   a. without taking a vote
   b. when nobody's looking
   c. in Idaho
   d. relentlessly, without regard for God's wrath

10. Business and pleasure ____ .
    a. both require rigorous training
    b. take place in public

   c.   each contain eight letters

   d.   are difficult for poor people

11.   A smart businessman never travels without _____.
- a.   a satchel full of colorful trinkets, nylons, and Hershey bars
- b.   cares
- c.   confirmed reservations
- d.   his bodyguard

12.   To err is human, to forgive _____.
- a.   canine
- b.   occasionally useful
- c.   just such an error
- d.   divine, but who wants to be described that way?

II

1.   I believe the following to be most true of myself:
- a.   If I just set my mind to it, I know I can do anything. No, really. Honest.
- b.   I don't think there are any important character limitations that people are just born with. But if only my voice were deeper.
- c.   If I died, no one would know until the library tried to recover its overdue books.
- d.   Someone I've never met is trying to poison me.

2.   It no longer bothers me that
- a.   I won't be the next Albert Einstein.
- b.   I won't be the late Albert Einstein.
- c.   I'm not what my brother is.
- d.   life is so short.

3. Salvador Allende is
   a. a former Chilean president.
   b. a former Chilean bandleader.
   c. a former Chilean.
   d. out of the way.

4. The business of America is
   a. to strive for the commonweal and social good, right?
   b. business.
   c. America.
   d. Chile.

5. Do you own a dog?
   a. It depends what you mean by "dog."
   b. Not to my knowledge.
   c. May I ask what this information is being used for?
   d. My counsel's phone number is 262–1000.

III

Read through the following list of potential human desires, keeping in mind that it is a *complete* list. Depending on the importance of each to you, write in the blank to the left a "1" for "not important at all," a "2" for "somewhat important," or a "3" for "more important ·than life itself."

_____ owning a pony with a bright red saddle
_____ financial security
_____ inner peace, of sorts
_____ having Liza or Andy tell me about rum-and-tonic at a party
_____ not suffocating

_____having my socks match
_____a sense of self-worth
_____just muddling through somehow
_____leading a life of quiet desperation
_____leading a life of noisy desperation
_____knowing the lyrics to every Burt Bacharach song by heart
_____having the respect of my broker
_____cinnamon graham crackers
_____sexual pleasure
_____meeting Sam Levenson
_____meeting God
_____being creative
_____convincing people I'm creative
_____maximizing profits
_____exploiting workers
_____exploding workers
_____working, working, working
_____understanding Roland Barthes
_____pronouncing Roland Barthes
_____winning the Nobel Prize for home safety

If this were just any quiz, a complex scoring system would follow. But this has been a test of a very different kind from what you're accustomed to: If you know your score already, then, brother, *you know the score.* On the other hand, if our radical new examination mode—that's right, with the correct and incorrect answers withheld from you—has caused you some anxiety, you may be in serious trouble. Deep, deep trouble. The kind of trouble a phone call home to your mom won't begin to solve, the sort of trouble a visit to your shrink or a heart-to-heart with your est facilitator will only make worse. There is a way out, but you'll have to be willing to work. Don't worry—it doesn't require any skill, but you'll have to read the rest of this book not just once, but two, three, and four times, making laborious marginal notations and keeping an index-card file of *General Insights* and *Really Applies to Me*. You're going to be required to strap bulky machinery to your body and place tape recorders under your pillow at night and rub special salves on your temples every morning. It's going to be rough. But if you want power—*real* power—there are no shortcuts. Superstition is by its nature elaborate.

But enough doom and gloom.

Yes.

Success can be yours.

But first, *you* must be *its*.

That's a mouthful, but what it means is simple: before you can control others, that *desire* for control must control *you*! An idle moment during your lunch break, a stray fancy as you lather up in the shower, an undisciplined thought twittering across your consciousness when you hear a distant car crash—and your lifetime of positive planning can be *undermined*.

It's as easy as pie to scale the breathtaking summits of Absolute Accomplishment—or Absolute Reward, anyway—but if you look down or away, you might get nauseated, or worse, disenchanted. Alden Shortford Pettypoint, the famous billionaire, once said: "If you want to be rich so you can live high on the hog, you'll never be rich—though you may live high on the hog." Because he was a billionaire, people have always treated this statement as if it made sense.

WHAT IS SUCCESS, ANYWAY?

Everybody knows what success is.

YOUR STANCE
FOR SUCCESS

In the Middle Ages people believed success was governed by *good luck charms* and *talismans* like rabbits' feet or horseshoes. Today we know that for the ignorant claptrap it was. Today we know that success is controlled by *little books* like this one. Silliness like walking around ladders or knocking on wood has been superseded by scientific techniques of memorized body language, symbolic aggression, and clothing stratagems. Success is no more related to merit than beauty is to mere good looks.

However, what's past is history, and you want to delve into the future, so let us proceed to some concrete platitudes. First, the *secret of success*—what we are about to reveal to you for less than the cost of a good pair of earmuffs—is this:

It's all in your mind.

Amazing, isn't it? But wait. Before you charge out and begin tearing up the world as we know it, let us state that another way:

Success depends on your attitude.

Let us review. First we said this about success:

It's all in your mind.

Then we said it another way:

Success depends on your attitude.

Or, in other words:

Success depends on your posture.

Yes, your *posture*. These maxims are not offered lightly. They have a very serious *meaning,* as a quick check of any dictionary will attest.

Your *Stance for Success* is your armor against humiliation—after all, it's escape from humiliation you want more than accomplishment itself—and your body is your weapon against the universe, whose governing principle is to hinder your personal desire to own two homes and a six-foot-wide television screen.

Many people ask what the Stance for Success is. Others ask why God allows evil, or how to keep eggs fresh without refrigeration. All of these are valid questions, but for now, bearing in mind the need for sharpening your outlook to a razor-narrow edge, let us concentrate on the first.

> *Your Stance for Success is the way you, you know,* stand, *your posture.*

Just as bullies and sissies have different postures, winners (you are one) and losers (everybody else) have distinct ways of carrying themselves. It sounds like charm school, but the effects can be nothing short of monumental. Of course, your Stance for Success doesn't just mean the way you are when you're standing up. It also means the way you dance, eat, sit, even lie down—all *as if* you were standing up.

Does this mean the on-the-make executive is always tense? Yes, you should be tense, but let's assign a healthier, researched-sounding euphemism to it:

> *Reserve unhappiness energy.*

By prudently using *reserve unhappiness energy* (your R.U.E.), you can propel yourself along like a high-speed racecar on a crash course with Success. First and foremost, though, remember that here as in all things, *you will be judged by the most trivial and unconscious of your actions.*

So it is not sufficient to manage a billion-dollar portfolio with virility and wisdom. You must demonstrate your worthiness in your every act—*especially* in your every act—and that includes the way you switch on a table lamp, the way you eat a cruller with your morning coffee, the way you shuffle through piles of autumn leaves deep in the forest all by yourself—*even if you think no one can see you.* The way you stub out a cigarette, the tautness of your shoelace, the way your body's cells assimilate oxygen—*nothing isn't crucial.*

THIS SOUNDS HELLISH

No one said it wouldn't be. But you knew perfectly well what success was when you started reading this, and it's too late to back out now.

BUT WAIT,
I WAS JUST THINKING—

Perhaps you were thinking to yourself: "That may be well and good for other people, but I just don't have it in me to dispassionately manipulate my fellow man, to ignore the quivering jowls and astonished, bewildered eyes of those who have just witnessed the severance of the common bonds of humanity."

We know you're thinking that, because those are the very words spoken to us by a former client of ours shortly before his conversion to our method and subsequent appointment to the vice-presidency of a prestigious multinational conglomerate whose initials are household words. In fact, we learned recently that he was the odds-on favorite for the chairmanship at the time of his wife's unfortunate breakdown and his own attendant suicide.

We've heard it all! "I just couldn't fire my old Army bunkmate with no severance pay when I know his mother is going senile and his wife's pregnant with my baby." We've heard it. "I just couldn't dissolve the chain of drugstores that includes the neighborhood shop still managed by old Pop McGillicuddy—the man who gave me my very first job—simply as a tax write-off, especially when I know his wife is pregnant with my baby." We've heard that. "I just couldn't frame my loyal protégé as a corporate spy when he is my child and doesn't know it." But every one of these slackers eventually did their duties. And when they finished with our training—training that is now the basis for this very book—*they wanted to.*

Thousands of confused souls have stumbled through our doors, helpless pawns in a game they didn't begin to understand, only to march out seven hours later, proud foot soldiers eager to manipulate the corporate kings and queens to serve their own newly realized interests.

And while not an easy transformation to make, it isn't impossible either. For most of you, the task will demand simply scraping away, like so much dime-store lacquer, the yellowing layers of concern and sensitivity so hastily applied to your character in reflective moments, or the late 1960s. Why, you can see it happening already, all around you, in today's shifting diction: "share," "therapeutic," and "meaningful experience" are being replaced by clipped, ascetic declaratives, such as "I have no problem with that" and "not to my knowledge." It's all part of the ongoing diffusion of the Bob Haldeman School of Mormonlike Functional Prose, replacing communication with data transference. You need only slough off your now-brittle, outmoded skin to allow the serpent to reemerge—renewed and refreshed—uncoiled and groveling along the path to success.

WHAT'S SNAKES GOT TO DO WITH IT?

The point is that nobody, if he or she is prepared to work hard enough, lacks the raw material to go the distance in this game. You don't have to be extraordinary. Life has proven, time and time again, that unusual gifts are liabilities. That macho high school stud has just drunk away his last hopes with a minor-league farm team in Rochester, while the class brain just yesterday picked off twelve pedestrians with a Winchester semiautomatic from some Sunbelt parapet. Their day has come and gone. Yours is just dawning.

DRESSED TO KILL

Beware of all enterprises that require new clothes, and not rather a new wearer of clothes.
—Henry David Thoreau

It's a truth too banal to resist repeating here that clothing separates man from the animals. True, we (i.e., man) may have art museums and symphonies and libraries, but without clothes we would not be admitted to any of these places. We would, in fact, be chased away by the doorman, probably with a broom, just as if we were a stray dog or raccoon, and in no time we would be living in wallows beside railroad tracks and eating fish skeletons out of ash bins.

Rather than pursue this unappetizing fancy any further, let us consider instead the singular importance of clothing in all human transactions, which for our purposes refer to getting ahead in business. Experience shows that men are judged by what they wear; our Fashion Consultants at the Success Clinic have helped to acquit defendants in felony trials who were not merely guilty but had committed scores of crimes to which the court was oblivious.

A well-chosen tie can inspire confidence, win affection, and, if it is the proper shade of rare Brazilian blue, induce instant madness in any beholder. Many undeserving men and women could be in exalted positions for which they were entirely unqualified, if only they knew how to use their neckties aggressively. Example: physicist Albert Einstein was long recognized as "smart" by his colleagues, but his sloppy, careless style of dress prevented him from winning any truly topflight jobs. Admittedly, he won a Nobel Prize and changed the face of science forever, but his income could have been trebled by a crisper haircut and a Princeton club tie.

But why dwell on failure? There'll be plenty of time for that later. It's a fact that tonsorial chicanery can jettison even a worthy man into the boardroom, though it may require dressing him like a Western Union messenger boy to get him past the receptionist. (At this point, some would-be kingpins will confess themselves amazed at how little relation there need be between the semblance of merit and merit itself. Men of a philosophical turn might say: "Don't judge me by my tie, but by my car!" And correct though they are, society doesn't permit you to have your car with you at all times, and it might be awkward to pass around photos of it at a conference with strangers. So it is your clothing which must say: "I am affluent and well-bred. I never have the hiccups, and I consummated my marriage with perfect ease.")

The key word in power-seeking fashion is *intimidation*. Your fellows are a superstitious lot, and anything short of sheets with spook eyes snipped out is shrewd game in exploiting their *need to be intimidated*. (Any psychiatrist will verify this phenomenon for a reasonable fee.)

We have already discussed your Stance for Success and How to Make Animal Magnetism and Grooming Work for You. Now that you're erect and tensed, your canines bared, your hair cut to stand on end, with a belligerent tang of urine about you—let's get some clothes on you!

First, always let research choose your clothing. No careful executive would dream of ordering lunch or naming his children until he had extensive reports and market analyses to guide his decisions, yet many leave the all-important job of outfitting themselves to wives, salesclerks, or in some pathetic cases, the parish aid society. Wives dress their husbands to look "nice," and we all know where nice guys finish. Salesclerks, ironically, do not know what clothes you should wear. If they did, they would wear them themselves and be elevated to the presidency of an international oil concern before their next weekly shave came due.

The problem with wives and salesclerks (and keep them distinct in your mind, or there'll be trouble) is that they think high-fashion clothing is the most desirable way to dress. Unfortunately, only very attractive men look good in high-fashion clothing, and even then only to other attractive men in high-fashion clothing. Our research shows that the style that gets promoted is conservative, college-educated, and well-to-do in appearance. True, some bosses are dwarfish self-made men, uneducated boors who despise all college graduates, all tall men, and the notion of promoting anyone, and if this describes your employer, there is nothing for you to do but bear his insults, because even if you dress and talk like him, he will still hate you. He will bait you at every turn, and yours will be a nightmarish life that even research can do nothing to ameliorate.

YOUR SUIT

Never take off your suit jacket. It is your throne and shield, your symbolic desk, your wall of authority and inflexibility. Remove the jacket and instantly your competitor will think, "Aha: Kindly Country Judge. Unaffected Bumpkin. Overheated Through Ineffectuality," and take advantage of you accordingly. This policy does not hold true for your overcoat, however. A man sitting at a business lunch in his London Fog suggests tacitly that he's retaining his option for a quick getaway, or is a devotee of queer meterological theories.

Bright colors worn at funerals will suggest you thrive on destruction, and others will stand out of your way. Conversely, the conservative black suit is so uncompromisingly Establishment that its power alienates some clients, particularly when it is worn with a black hood. Capes and shoulder holsters are fine, but better know how to use them unless you're very glib at recoveries (muffled gunshots can disconcert even a prealerted associate, and the pain of concealing your faux pas can be draining). Open jackets without vests are acceptable go-getter gear if you don't mind people assuming you're a basketball coach or a candidate for office.

Styles to beware of: anything you could play checkers on, or worse, Parcheesi; all broad horizontal stripes (these imply a history of incarceration); any suit that has detachable sleeves or buttons larger than you could conveniently swallow. With these considerations in mind, you are ready to have your suit fitted.

YOUR FITTING

Unless you're one of the lucky few men who are of average height, your suit will require some adjustments. Rather than

1   6

regard this as a nuisance, most executives prefer to think of the ordeal as one more chance to upset and berate the functionally helpless. Even if your new garment fits perfectly, insist on five or six fittings to make your perfectionism clear to these strangers who will never see you again. Contradict their recommendations concerning sleeve measurements by insisting your arms are of unequal lengths. Slip the tailor a ten and mention suavely, "I'm very particular about my socks." This will show you to be compulsive and paranoid, traits that prove your ambition and always elicit consideration from those dealing with you.

The best way to determine if your sleeves are the proper length is to let your arms hang casually at your sides. Now raise them slowly until they are parallel with the floor. Now lower them. Now raise them again. Faster. Lower them. Again. Faster. Begin to hum. Actually, the best way to detect overlong (or "Dopey") sleeves is to ask the tailor to name the number of fingers you are holding up. If he's right more often than not, the visibility is probably sufficient.

If you choose custom-made clothing, your most important concern will be ensuring that everyone knows that that's what it is. Most top executives arrange to be paged thus in whatever hotel or restaurant they're visiting: "Will the man with the full custom suit please see the bell captain?" Others remark casually that they are having their shirts taken out to accommodate the previous weekend's mosquito bites. In fact, the more physically anomalous you are (no arms, say), the more readily acknowledged custom-made clothes will be.

YOUR SHIRT

Remember, it's always acceptable to dress for the job you *want,* unless the position you seek is the monarchy. This is especially true in the white-collar world of shirts and the men who stuff them. The more luxurious and impractical the shirt, the more clearly transmitted your intention to occupy a superfluous situation at the highest echelons.

Shirts without pockets tell strangers: "I don't have to do paperwork, so I don't need a pencil pocket." Long-sleeve shirts, especially on hot days, say, "I'm not a grocer or a mechanic—I sit quietly in an air-conditioned room." Dress to emphasize how little physical effort is required of you—single-sleeve shirts that encase both arms (many great writers affect these later in life) demonstrate just how slight the labors incumbent upon you must be.

Beware of "bargains." A shirt may have a low initial (capital) cost, but it will be augmented over time by laundry bills and such, so what you must consider uppermost is the shirt's *eventual* cost (e.g., KICK ME embroidered across the back of a shirt may add hundreds of dollars to its initial cost). Many apparent good buys have unseen deficiencies of irregularities (pullovers with no hole for the head to go through), but occasional bargains do exist. Widows of recently deceased corporate officials usually feel painful nostalgia when confronted with their late spouse's wardrobe, and they generally give top value if you are persistent in your phone calls and offers. (But remember that no circumstance absolves you of the duty to haggle, if for no other reason than out of respect for the expectations of the dead.)

The white shirt, like the white lie, is always preferred for business. Tests have shown that of men dressed identically except for a white shirt (the other wore strings of sheep intestine under his sports jacket), the white shirt is given favored placement in elevators, lifeboats, and revolving doors. Leave imagination to your wry phone-answering machine messages (even then it is a risk), and stick to the virtuous blank of pristine Brooks Brothers. A white shirt is like a movie screen on which those you meet will project the home movies of their own crudely shaped, untested ideals. In a world where all statements are dangerous, the buttoned lip of a button-down shirt guarantees discreet sartorial silence.

YOUR TIE

In an experiment conducted at a leading New York resturant, two hundred chimpanzees were sent through the front door right as the lunch rush was beginning. Of these, one hundred wore neckties and one hundred did not. None of them were seated, of course, but 40 percent fewer people complained about the smell of the chimpanzees wearing ties.

This dramatizes the importance that the proper necktie can have for the man devoted to getting ahead in the World According to Others. Since your suit and shirt have been strategically chosen to be as conformist and undistinguished as possible, your neckwear is your last chance to assert your individuality, but don't get foolish. Solid colors are always trustworthy since it is natural to assume that what is dull must be true, so let that snoring solidity sound through in your choice of ties. Stripes suggest double-talk, plaids a kind of dizzying subterfuge, and as for paisley, well, paisley is like throwing your client down a flight of stairs and (if the colors are gaudy enough) hurling imprecations after him.

HOW TO TIE A TIE

The Tower of London Knot
(adjustable in the extreme)

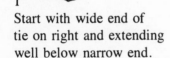

1
Start with wide end of
tie on right and extending
well below narrow end.

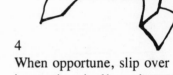

4
When opportune, slip over
inattentive rival's neck.

2
Cross wide end over narrow
and bring up through loop.

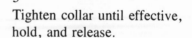

5
Tighten collar until effective,
hold, and release.

3
Bring wide end around narrow, down behind, and up
through again.

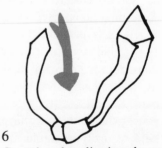

6
Complete by slipping down
through back stairs and ex-
iting unnoticed. Discard tie.

The merits of executive wit have been dismissed earlier, and neckties with anything akin to "plot"—hula girls, marlins in mid-flight, teen boys at tennis, and the like—are likely to fatigue your luncheon companions with the insistence that they read at the table. Something lulling, in a solid aquatic color, will more readily dispose your associate to the compliant drowse that best complements the illegal and usurious recommendations you are about to make.

Club ties have to be chosen with the utmost care, particularly since it's likely that you have never been in a club. Some perfectly respectable Ivy League patterns secretly betoken a ritualistic cult that expects its adherents to murder each other on sight. And just as an imprudently specific tartan pattern on a scarf can subject you to hours of tedious conversation with passersby of Scottish descent, so too with ties. If you select the colors of the Cambridge Debating Society because the stripe goes well with your shaving scars, be prepared to accept the consequences, since anyone you meet who recognizes something so obscure is bound to be both pedantic and argumentative, and will engage you in a discussion of Common Market tariff rates in short order.

Now as to the bow tie, the problem child in the neckwear family. One of the challenges of recent fashion is that clothes no longer necessarily make direct statements; they are often, in fact, "witty," or even downright ironic. The bow tie, sadly, seems to be satiric, and, even sadder, satiric of an insignificant subject. The man who wears bow ties is either a very old prig (there are few such left in business) or one who takes the trouble to show his disapproval of such harmless characters by satirically imitating them. (This latter variety of man is abundant in the modern business world, particularly among the youngish.)

Yes, now and then a true lover of "all centuries but this and every country but his own" emerges in a crowd of acquaintances you have meticulously limited to acquaintanceship, and such a man wears a bow tie. Like a superlative Gilbert and Sullivan performer, however, he will be encouraged to continue by people who feel no obligation to attend themselves.

YOUR HAT

The pinnacle of your business wear, geographically if not emotionally, is your hat. Hats are like sheaths on daggers— they cover one's raw essence. But if you must put a condom on your aura, choose your headgear with delicacy. We recommend a coal miner's helmet with the light kept *fully ablaze*. The glare from the lamp will cause your associates to wince and look away—and unconsciously to associate you with its blinding, inscrutable power. Also, the light will obscure your own features, making you mysterious, inaccessible, even magical. Remember always: *They need to be intimidated*.

YOUR HAIR,
OR SOMEONE'S

The shape of the head, which is well-known as the determinant of people's opinions of each other, can be counteracted dramatically by intelligent use of hair, be it original or acquired. Let's face the facts: Thin faces look effeminate, fat faces look inefficient, normal faces look talentless, and monstrous faces look monstrous. In fact, as far as business is concerned, you may safely assume that every face is repellent to every other. Still, a haircut may help confuse the signals long enough to allow you to make your move.

Bangs seldom inspire awe in one's associates, and even a Kennedyesque boyish charm is not advanced by a cowlick. Youthfulness, while desirable, is limited in a business sense to the blush that accompanies the apparent age of thirty. However, neither is it a good idea to affect aging. Spray-on gray for your hair will make you resemble an inept high school production of *You Can't Take It with You*, or more pointedly, *Death of a Salesman*. Glasses will visually increase your age (in addition to sparing you the occasional punch in bars), and a few leisurely months of reading in the dark will entitle you to sport a pair legitimately.

Most of the world, however, does not have to grapple with the challenges of prolonged youthfulness, and the hair supply is the outstanding traditional odometer of Time's winged chariot. Baldness—the crown of failure, the satanic glittering prize, the unwelcome country from whose bourn no traveler returns without falsifying his passport—is like life itself, insofar as it can be disguised but never remedied. Acquire a hairpiece, if it appeals to you. After all, toupee is no longer a dirty word, though it is still a very funny one. If you have adopted children, you may already know the queasy sense of semi-ownership it provides.

What about dyeing your hair, you ask. Well, what about it, homo?

SHOES

In any color other than black, shoes, like limousines, look like the property of a pimp. Slips-ons are unacceptable outside of private school faculties, even ones with false shoelaces attached to give the "tie-shoes" effect. If you are to play tennis with a client, wear tennis shoes (thousands of Iona College seniors failed to do this during a recent practice seminar). If you are to go bowling with a client, dump him.

HANDKERCHIEFS

A letter from a leading would-be business figure dramatizes the timeless handkerchief question: "I have heard the hand-kerchief is passé, but when my client sneezes and gets, well, a little drippy, frankly, I hate to say, *'Here, let me offer you my wad of Kleenex.'* "

We recommend that you exploit his mistake by saying, "Wow, gross, I can't believe what I'm seeing!" and offering nothing. This does not require a handkerchief.

These fashion secrets must of course be kept from your numerous rivals. For them we recommend a terrible book entitled *Dress Bright So As to Look Right*. This volume advocates such unwise practices as wearing fish on Fridays and exposing interesting surgical scars. One chapter of the book is entirely devoted to the indispensability of jodhpurs. This is the book to give each of your competitors as a Christmas present, or, more effectively, let them "catch" you reading it in the staff supply room some afternoon. Before long they will be coming to work in enormous Day-Glo muumuus, and you will be on your way up the corporate ladder.

THE
OBJECTS
OF YOUR
AFFECTION

---

*He who possesses most must be
most afraid of loss.*
—Leonardo da Vinci

Every profession has its indispensable tools. Once upon a time, before newspaper reporters wrote their stories on television screens and people got their news only from television, *tools* were the province of grizzled men in caulk-stained overalls. Tools were hard and fine things, designed specifically and exclusively for defeating wood and metal and rock. They hung on wall-sized pegboards (in your home) or rested on dusty benches (elsewhere). A distinct caste in the kingdom of inanimate objects, and when Dad or the plumber said, "Son, this is a *dependable tool*," there was no ambiguity about his meaning (unless—and this had best include most of you—your father was not a plumber).

But the 1960s, the 1970s, and the *Whole Earth Catalog* intervened to blur this simple picture. The *Whole Earth* creators had a peculiarly dichotomized view of life: There

---

exists on one hand Seekers of a Better Way, and on the other, *tools*. Period. Anyone (or thing) that is neither a dissatisfied former drug user nor a buyer of windmill kits is a tool. The last decade and a half brought tools out of the closet in every sense (and indeed the closet itself became a "tool for space definition"). Astrology became a tool. Hand-operated granaries and mountain-climbing equipment are now more tools than ever before. Psychotherapy and its New Age rivulets (see next chapter) are tools now, as are massage, leveraging money, Herman Kahn, *Fortune* magazine, LSD, real estate maneuvers, old farmers, and photographs of placentas and the moon. All tools. All the world's a workshop, and all the men and women merely planers.

Just as the C.I.A. discovered it could profit from a *selective* use of bohemia's sacraments—mind-altering substances seemed like nifty operative's equipment to Langley, but incense and paisley bandannas proved less useful as counterintelligence devices—the corporate world too found merit, or at least comfort, in a discriminating Whole Earth way of looking at their mission. To be sure, few Manhattan merchandising vice-presidents actually moved to northern Maine, built an earthen hut for shelter, and tried to eke out an existence on kale and good vibes; it was discovered to be difficult, besides, to impress livestock with catchy slogans and three-screen multimedia presentations. But the everything's-a-tool notion has seeped into the business ken and stayed.

Suddenly, a life spent initialing memos, calculating cost per thousand, and meeting to plan meetings—all the once-dreary effluvia of life behind a desk—takes on a gritty new twang. No longer pointy-headed pencil pushers you: All the time you've been using *tools* and never realized it! With a major portion of the material world redefined as a collection of tools, that word-processing junior exec is miraculously transformed. He becomes Superworkingman, with the pride of a craftsman in his kit of interpersonal *tools*, communications *tools*, managerial *tools*, and even (with a throbbing array of lightweight metal and microprocessors) real old-fashioned *hardware*, tools as we know them! And all of this cleaned-up proletarian ruggedness at three times the salary, and *without* the inconvenience of unsightly plastic safety goggles or trade union dues.

It was Marx who said that the tools a man uses shape him. Aside from the relatively isolated instances of chainsaw suicides among lumberjacks, the truth of this maxim may be hard to grasp. Its portent for us of the modern age is less literal, perhaps, but no less profound.*

THE COMPUTER

Computers did not exist at all in the nineteenth century. The industrial capitalists of Marx's day were obliged to rely for their computational needs on huge, steam-powered abacuses. These were great, rumbling contraptions of pig iron and teak, each filling an entire two-story building. A task that is today routinely accomplished in seconds by businessmen all over the country—computing the "rating" of a particular episode of a TV program, for instance—took months and even years of backbreaking work to complete as recently as the 1870s. Fuel and raw materials were plentiful and cheap in those days, of course, and there was no shortage of desperate immigrant labor eager to spend eighteen-hour days stoking the hungry furnaces of the industrial

---

* And notice, too, how we of the modern age are able to draw from sources as eclectic as Marx and Mallarmé, all in a book about business. Call it synergy. Call most things synergy, in fact.

abacuses. But even the simplest arithmetic problem was a Herculean labor. With the full eight-man work team toiling expertly and furiously—the brawny *countermeisters* resetting the heavy wooden spheroids, the foreman working the big steam lever, and the sooty stokers shoveling in mountains of anthracite—it took all of June 1853, to come up with the solution to 259 minus 133. To derive the cube root of 729, say, might engage a whole factory of these nine-ton behemoths working night and day throughout an entire computing season. It was a sorry, backward time, when the only tools of business were those tended by big ferocious men who'd never heard of cost accounting and who depreciated fast.

A technological marvel in its time, the only abacus we are likely to encounter today is one of the pocket-sized digital models crafted by miniaturization wizards in a formerly Axis nation. This is the age of computers. The world has had a love affair with the electronic brain from the moment thirty years ago when the first clunky UNIVAC sashayed into our lives. And the old girl did serve her purpose. But there were lines of flashier, cannier computers waiting to take her place in our hearts. According to a professor friend of ours, what took the first computers an *hour* to perform can now be accomplished faster by a bag of dirt or a pile of glass shards. A machine that in 1954 cost two million dollars can now be built so cheaply that computer manufacturers will *pay you* to take one.

Unfortunately, many congenitally skeptical businessmen still think that buying a computer won't immediately solve all their problems. They are wrong. Why do so many businesses fail? Why did that little pizza pie shop down the block declare bankruptcy last year? Because they didn't own a computer. It's as simple as that. "But wait," you say. "Hold on there. Computers aren't magic. Some business problems just aren't suited to computerized solutions. Computers can't do everything." Yes they are, yes they are, yes they can. Computers *are* magic, literally. Competitors may have been conspiring to withhold this valuable information from you, but now you know the truth, printed here in a book (so you can say, "I read it in a book"). Buy a computer, plug it in, start throwing around words like "software," "interface," and "on-line," and nearly all of your knotty business difficulties will be solved.

THE DESK

Purchasing a huge, impressive, mahogany desk will not *immediately* untangle the web of problems plaguing your business. Many otherwise naturally dubious businesspeople say, "Wait a second. Hold your horses. I've heard that all you have to do is get a big, expensive desk, plug it in, and presto! all cash-flow difficulties, all price-earnings lags are solved, like that." True, *in theory*. But have you ever tried to plug in a desk? Especially one of those rosewood models that run on European current? No; a desk alone is no panacea.

But a desk is not without utility. And here the instinct for sheer size is, as in most things, correct. (Flatness is also important. A desktop designed to reproduce the topography of Wyoming, say, may be stylish but can present real problems when all your pens and paper clips tumble into an inconvenient Rocky Mountain valley, and the stucco desks so popular among Arizona businessmen can create difficulties in writing legibly.) A would-be executive's desk cannot be too large. Before you deserve to hope to be Chairman of the Board, you must be chairman of *your* board, your desk, your own personal playing field. A proper desk should be at least as long as you are tall, and twice as many feet wide as you have children. Your office is little more than a cubbyhole? Resolutely ignore those space restrictions: "They" may control the size of your office, but *you* are the master of your desk's dimensions.

Can't this obsession with expansiveness get out of hand, reach an absurd point of diminishing returns? No one calls Harold Geneen (not his real name) inappropriate or absurd. Harold is the executive vice-president of a firm that manufactures first-aid gear for the House of Representatives, the largest in its field, and he attributes his undisputed fast-track success to one *thing*: his enormous mahogany desk. "You know the old saying," Harold once remarked to us, "about genius being two percent inspiration and ninety-eight percent how big your desk is. Well, I may be no genius, but I've come a long way from selling secondhand tourniquets door to door. And you can bet that even today, every extra buck goes right back into *that* baby." Geneen nods affirmatively and a bit protectively toward The Desk.

Harold doesn't store cash *inside* his wooden wonder: he invests in it, constantly making capital improvements, building on additions. And indeed, he couldn't pack away savings there even if he wanted to, for his desk lacks drawers entirely. Studies have confirmed Geneen's instinctual wisdom in this connection, proving that excessive personal storage space is perceived as lower class, unbecoming, and worse. "Pure *desk*," Harold snaps with gusto.

In fact, it is pure desk exclusively—one vast, nut-brown plane—that occupies Geneen's 450-square-foot office. No Mies chairs, no hidden bar, no family photographs or diplomas. Just yards of solid desk, wall to wall. Visually breathtaking and, more important, psychologically off-putting to visitors, Geneen's desk is the apotheosis of effective office furniture. It would be the foolhardy client or associate who'd sneer or giggle as the master of this desk scampered across its polished, naked surface to greet them at the door.

THE TELEPHONE

The trouble with symbols of power is that different things impress different people. Unlike the stripes of military ranking or the number of chickens in a rooster's roster, there are no unmistakable ways to amass proof of your success, or evidence of what you would like others to call success, anyway. You may invite someone to peruse your gratuitous, cheek-to-cheek platinum fillings, and he may look you in the mouth and still think, *so what*?

Power expresses itself by coldly showering inconvenience on others, and the most potent wand of that intrusiveness is the telephone. The telephone is like a gift-boxed token of how much the world needs you, its ring like the plaintive chirp of a baby robin eager to see some worms. Every time the phone is for you, it means that someone somewhere *can't quite go on* until he consults you. Many executives instruct their secretaries to call them regularly, throughout the day, just to say in different voices, "Keep going! Good work!" Some executives limit these interruptions to whenever they have an important visitor in their office, to demonstrate by wasting time how much in demand they themselves are. This trick may be played on you, but in such an event feel free to regard what is ingenious in yourself as pathetic and craven in your adversary.

What makes the phone an effective power symbol? Size? Large phones can make their users look infantile. Number of buttons? The truly *arrived* potentate does no physical labor at all, and that should include digital juggling of calls. Simplicity of spirit is impossible for success, but simplicity of veneer is indispensable. No, the measure of success, we have decided, is to be the *number* of telephones.

All those phones don't have to be connected, but the more of them you can fit in your office, the better. Pile them high (but neatly) in every corner. An armory of reasons to live will surround you. Imagine the exciting cuckoo-clock-shop effect when all the phones start ringing at once! Most of them will be your secretary, playing her master control panel like a ghoul at the organ, but your visitor will know only that you are more sought after than the Philosopher's Stone, and he will respect you for it. Earning respect and being respectable can be two different occupations.

This abundance of telephones must be handled with taste, of course. All your phones should be in the same or compatible colors; the Princess style and the Mickey Mouse should be avoided, possibly even decried in public. And *always* make sure to apologize for how busy the phones make you, smiling with ingenuous bewilderment, as if the rigors of greatness have been thrust upon you by the sheer impetus of your merit. Involuntary popularity is the purest, since it does not exist in real life.

What, however, of the man who actually expects and receives numerous phone calls? If you are so fortunately afflicted, make sure the world knows. If you have a limousine, you will doubtless have a phone installed in it; limousine sensibilities include a restless taste for optional equipment. A lesser exec we know (but do not acknowledge on the street) had a phone installed near his regular seat on the morning bus, but complications have arisen involving constant "check-up" calls from the driver's highly jealous wife. To avoid such skirmishes, stick to installing phones in private vehicles (bicycles, life rafts, tunnel-of-love cars) or, best of all, have an incoming calls system surgically implanted. A first-rate barber will be able to disguise the tiny aerial.

Now, finally, an answer to the dilemma that obsessed Herbert Marcuse during his last years—when and why to put someone on hold. Titillation through frigidity was perfected by young women in the antebellum South, and that principle has been ideally applied in the hold button. *I want you*, it says, *but be patient*. Beneath its mechanical silence is the further implication, *I am worth waiting for*. The old, monogamous one-man-one-phone-call framework has fallen away as resoundingly as the country store or dating between adults. People want to be *reached*, to inwardly score popularity points, but they want the option of deferring or discouraging the contact itself. For them, the hold button is a latter-day dance card for the daily masquerade ball of business.

On a less purple note, the act of putting someone on hold is to mortify him by assuming his time is subservient to yours. This is one of the risks of making phone calls, and for that reason it is best never to make them. A true success should never have to make a call, anyway. The mountain certainly didn't phone Muhammad. One powerful executive we knew ostentatiously installed phones in his protected inner office that could receive calls, but were not wired for outgoing ones. He was much admired and is still highly thought of, years after his death in a wastebasket fire.

THE ROLODEX

In the business world, the truly savvy have had a lot of experience with Rolodexes and no longer seek opportunities to twirl them round and round just for fun. Try to use the Rolodex with dispatch and indifference, as if it were little more than a booklet containing the same information.

When not in operation, which card should it be left at? This is a delicate matter. To simply leave it at a card with the name of a powerful person or celebrity implies that you do not know that person well enough to know his number and address by heart.

A borderline famous person is all right, but it is unbusinesslike to provide an answer key on a later card or even upside down on the same card. We recommend a number not directly affiliated with work, but suggesting an impossibly comprehensive life outside the office—"Sotheby Parke Bernet" is a pretty good choice, or "N.Y.A.C.— fencing level." Famous restaurants are too easy, but the chef at one is permissible.

Although truly famous people are out, their spouses, biographers, or principal detractors are fine choices. "Elsa the Lion" is unconvincing; "Joy Adamson Estate" is okay; "Born Free the Lion" is a real mistake.

Amassing the right card file for you takes years of polishing and pruning. But one successful San Francisco tycoon, justly famous for the subtle effectiveness of his Rolodex, features the following H entries:

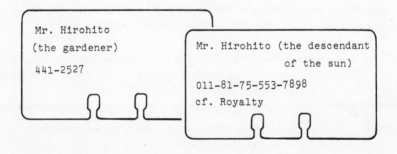

```
Mr. Hirohito
(the gardener)
441-2527
```

```
Mr. Hirohito (the descendant
                of the sun)
011-81-75-553-7898
cf. Royalty
```

PENCILS, PENS,
AND DICTATING MACHINES

Pencils are used by blue-collar workers, children below the fourth grade, and all other people when they have run out of typewriter ribbon, ink, green ink, lipstick, and blood. When white-collar workers cannot avoid using pencils, they use poorly disguised metal-plated versions called "mechanical pencils," but they still don't brag about it. In fact, the pencil, like the umbrella, is one of the few categories of consumer products that Western society will not dignify with recognition as private property.

Ballpoint pens are slightly different. People will, without blushing, speak of "my pen." Polite people use ballpoint pens in their everyday affairs, to conclude contracts, to charge lunches, to leave notes to their abandoned children, or to sign legislation into law. All the same, ballpoint pens are available at all strata of society and impress no one, not even Soviet tourists, although there has been some confusion on this point. Pens are not a good status symbol. Expensive pens look like bar mitzvah gifts, and cheap pens do not have any camp value, even the ones with pinup girls in disappearing nighties.

Dictating machines are plainly the correct tool. Dictating machines will not leak all over your pocket or advertise a driving school *que habla español*. But more than that, they establish that you are a man with no time for perfunctory workaday instrumentalities like written language. We recommend purchasing the tapes that provide a background of muffled traffic noises and clinking glasses.

Warning: Audio electronics is a rapidly developing field, perhaps a bit too unpredictable to provide a sturdy foundation for a status symbol. We believe at this writing that the dictating machine will be a safe bet for several years, but as soon as you notice the United Parcel delivery man balancing a Dictaphone behind his ear, it will be time to buy an updated edition of this book.

THE BRIEFCASE

Simple and understated. Real leather. (If it's real it will smell like a sports car.) No scenarios from *Battlestar Galactica* should adorn the sides.

Should there be initials? The United States Department of State has formulated its entire African policy around gaining access to Rhodesian chrome, which is used secondarily in ornamenting discos and Chryslers, but primarily in the manufacture of just such initials for briefcases sold to snazzy young Italian-Americans. We think the government knows what it's doing, but you should have three burned-in initials on your briefcase.

THE

ME TOO

DECADE

Man derives his moral sense from the social feelings which are instinctive in the lower animals.
　　　　　　—Charles Darwin

As we say good-bye to the 1970s—or, more likely, unfeelingly say *"ciao,* good buddy'' prefatory to sucking up to the 1980s—it's time to take inventory. And this is one time you can't order your earnest young stockperson to handle the task for you.

The last ten years saw the proliferation of all manner of psychology, ideology, mysticism, and most relevant here, plain old mumbo jumbo. Now, at the outset of this showroom-new decade, it's time for you to use this parcel of mental gewgaws to the hilt and to your own selfish ends. If during the seventies Americans sought to dress the wounds of materialism and competition with spiritual salves, during the eighties you can profit by picking their emotional scabs.

These diverse philosophies and pseudosciences that have reshaped a generation of mass-market consumers have also transferred their simplistic authority to a host of new business methods. Californians now hold preliminary legal hearings in hot tubs, and New Yorkers routinely expect open-access cable TV discussions to precede the granting of any corporate loan.

The predominant trend is toward *enlightened ruthlessness,* applying the wisdom of the ages wherever it can be construed to excuse temporal venal ambitions. Just as one can Meditate to Better Racketball, so can modern execs Zen Their Way to Power through scrupulously advertising a less-competitive-than-thou superiority. Some adherents complain that to win by not wanting to win, however, requires them actually *not* to want to—a bind comparable to the folk-tale dilemma of the flying carpet that will fly only if the owner really doesn't care if it does or not. Others prefer retreading Christian thought, and learn to Pray More Dynamically, or arrange to be born again very noisily, to show their determination and the frightening depth of their resolves.

Mainly, though, *psychology* has reared its misshapen head in business theory. The corridors of Everyman's mind, once the strict province of sideshow memory prodigies, are now open to observation and development by any with patience and a magazine article telling them what to see. By becoming a ''people'' person, an executive no longer causes accidental damage to the lives of those with whom he comes in contact. His new sensitivity enables him to calculate and to direct the damage with unprecedented accuracy. After thousands of years, men are no longer strangers. Unfortunately (some would say), they are by no means friends.

APPLIED FREUD

Children instinctively know how to hurt each other's feelings without ever reading a psychology book, but some adults allow that precious faculty to atrophy. Grownups, after all, cannot ordinarily resort to a high tree limb after taunting a peer for overweight. The study of the subconscious—or, in your colleagues' case, the semiconscious—is of great help to those whose natural thoughtlessness has been crippled. Freud and his descendants have left a body of work that many on-the-risers find as useful as the bad kid in your neighborhood found paperback accounts of Apache atrocities.

Freud à la Machiavelli requires extensive physical props. If the chairs in your reception area have undersized oval seats, your adversaries (and putative comrades) will enter your office unwittingly shaken and humbled by the subtle reminder of potty training they have just so dimly endured. A maternal-looking receptionist who praises others in the waiting room (and whom you have expressly hired for this purpose), but ignores Your Chosen Target, will promote his sense of unworthiness. A softly lit, womb-shaped reception area is not a bad idea either; when clients are ejected from it into your presence, the ritualized birth trauma they experience leaves them limp and acquiescent.

Your own office (or "den of inequity") should be maximized for subliminal aggression. Camouflaged furniture (i.e., upholstered to match the floor) will be much tripped over, delicately reminding visitors that they are on your turf, and less in control than you are. Few people will be impressed by "Dark Daddy" symbols, such as desktop meerschaum pipes or clipper ship paperweights, since most of them know from lesser guidebooks to strew their own cubicle with the very same flotsam of the Masculine Mystique. However, there is still fresh intimidation to be had from savage tabletop plants, highly polished cylindrical sculptures, and discreet piles of moist cattle bones.

By making the doorway to your office only two feet high, you can insure that the caller will enter not only with hat in hand, but on hands and knees. Similarly, a respected corporate chief in Boston conducts his business in absolute darkness, lighting one ominous candle only when signing purchase contracts, a practice that epitomizes the Ivy League will-to-alienate.

When it comes to humbling your adversary, it helps no end to tailor your attack to whatever you can learn about his or her infant years and prevailing neuroses. Just as you customize your clothing, customize your skulduggery. For instance, suppose an unwanted baby survives abandonment in a trash can and grows up to eminence as a maritime lawyer, albeit your rival. Imagine his uneasiness when you seat him in such a receptacle when he comes for consultations, while you blandly observe how challenging "designer furniture" can be, especially these "High-Tech" foofaraws. "Static on the intercom" can be your excuse for piped-in rat chitterings, and you can arrange a subtle odor of vegetable rot to tinge the room. A long-suppressed sense of loneliness will well up and unman him, enabling you to write your own ticket if you will just give him a hug and brush away the lettuce scraps with which you have connived to surround him.

Or suppose your files show that a troublesome client was a bed-wetter at summer camp, decades ago. Show him to a seat and yawn visibly. He will reflexively imitate you, at which point you should ask if he enjoyed his nap. Bewildered, he will protest that he does not recall falling asleep. You give a wan smile and proceed with business. After a few seconds, the client will sense a dampness in his chair seat (since the cushion on it is a laden sponge specially placed there) and will begin his inevitable collapse. You evince nothing but indulgent indifference, possibly referring to him as a "homesick little fella" as you outline the report before you, or venturing a solicitous glance at his trousers. Before long he will be as malleable as the once-and-future toddler many men and women were born to be.

From here, other possibilities are obvious: rubber tarantulas, tape loops of malevolent laughter, coffee meetings on sickeningly high ledges, bathroom doors with a disconcerting tendency to lock from the outside—the tactics are as myriad as the varieties of submerged human discomfort. There are, admittedly, a few benign ways to appeal to others' attachments to past emotional events; there have been several instances of executives dressing up as their client's favorite childhood toy or stuffed animal, to lucrative results. However, shame is a more volatile commodity than nostalgia, and has built many more empires. Even Freud knew that.

PROFIT
FROM YOUR DREAMS

Ever since Joseph used his dreams about cows to forecast Egyptian business prospects for the Pharaoh, opportunistic men have tried to wring from their sleeping fantasies benefits for their waking hours. Dreams may not foretell the future, but they do illuminate the present, which, finally, is simply the menu for whatever the Fates have on ice for you elsewhere, be it champagne or crow.

Many businessmen will say, "But I don't dream," and many more will say, "But I can't sleep," and if you are either or both of these men, dream analysis is as theoretical for you as unicorn grooming. However, if you do sleep, and perchance dream as well, you have a lucrative source of input about your current situation as close as your own head. If you can pay attention while unconscious, you can learn a lot about yourself, and at considerably less expense than hiring a biographer.

Consider this example taken from a transcription of a dream one of our clients had during a particularly stultifying session of our Success Clinic:

> *I am at home with my wife when slowly I realize the furniture is sinking into the floor, as if it were quicksand. Lamps, bookcases, and our new magazine rack all disappear beneath the deep-pile carpet. I call to my wife, but she seems not to hear. I tell her to get the children out of the house, but she is already slipping down into the carpet herself. Somehow I escape.*

This man's highly developed sense of self-righteousness and hysteria led us to recommend he become a market analyst. This we assume he did, because we never heard from him after the seminar ended, which leads us to conclude that he is now a great enough success to ignore his old friends.

Another dream that is commonplace among people who can be so described themselves is this nightmare:

> *I stop at the newsstand before a big conference and the old guy who sells me a pack of Certs points out that I'm not wearing any clothes. Covering myself with my attaché as best I can, I take the elevator up to the penthouse offices where the*

*conference is to be. Stares and murmurs greet my
arrival, and I debate whether to make an excuse
or to brave it out proudly. Instead, I burst into
tears. I know my career is finished. I have this
dream almost every night.*

The dangers of self-revelation are well-known, and
particularly in business it is inadvisable to be understood.
This dreamer's failure is not so much nudity (indeed, we are
all nude underneath) as it is vulnerability. Anyone experienced in adultery will add that although the unclothed body
seems to stand for honesty and self-exposure, one's real secrets, devious or otherwise, remain well-protected. The
troubled dreamer in this case must learn to ballyhoo honesty
and directness while never himself feeling intimidated by its
demands. He should endlessly worry what others think of
him, of course, but with a yeomanly effort he can make
himself so unknown that others will never possess sufficient
information on which to pass judgment.

A similar problem is reflected in this dream, which
many report having but few have seen in its uncut form:

*I somehow miss my stop on the commuter train
and continue into the wilds. Animals and foreign-
looking people fill the car, which seems suddenly
to spring with lush tropical vegetation. It gets
pitch-black outside, and a great wind begins to
shake the car. I feel a pitch and roll under my
feet, and realize the train is floating in space,
writhing, as it were, in a void. The animals and
foreigners grin to reveal sharpened teeth, and I
have only a wristwatch to barter my way out of
mealhood. I pass out, or wake up, as they circle
'round me.*

Anyone who has ever missed his stop on a homebound train knows that nothing like this happens. No incidents of cannibalism have been reported on the Long Island Rail Road, for instance, in over three years. Curiously, this dream is reported more often by Republicans than Democrats, though the latter group usually describe an interlude in which they offer the foreigners and animals money. In either case, such a dream bespeaks a xenophobia that would well suit a personnel director at a banking concern. Its conservatism suggests caution in foreign investments and a healthy distrust of excess, in this case, "going too far" on one's train. Storefront lawyers and international trouble-shooters should detect in this dream (should they have it) an unspoken desire to change careers, to seek localized power, where everyone they exploit will call them by their first names.

Sentimentality like that is rare but must be dealt with to maximize any individual's potential. A Pennsylvania executive dreamed so consistently of his old gray-haired mother he finally picked up the phone and sold her thousands of dollars worth of bogus insurance. Here is another dream whose profit-making possibilities may at first seem elusive:

> *I am not even in this dream. There is a large rock, several large rocks, in fact, sitting in a row. They're boulders, if you want to know the truth. The weather is overcast, and the rocks just sit there and sit there. Hours go by. The rocks are still there.*

Whoever has a dream like this is clearly the stuff of which great executive vice-presidents are made. Solidity, scrupulous attention to detail, and general satisfaction with the superficial are all traits that will rocket the man who knows how to use such gifts to a well-upholstered subordinate position. There is a further popular appeal to this personality, insofar as it generously dreams about subjects other than itself. While this may hinder it from absolute power, such self-effacement will be routinely advanced a great distance, the way innocuous-looking luggage breezes through customs.

Strangely, few would-be successes ever report having dreamed about money—piles of it, bags of it, or even rooms full of it. Since money most directly denotes power, why does it figure so slightly in dreamscapes? Consider this chimera, experienced in the fitful sleep of a New York broker:

> *Somehow I'm living on the Isle of Yap, where all the money is made of stone and cut into coins seven feet in diameter. I think my son was reading to me from Ripley's before I went to bed. Anyway, I have to open an account at the local savings bank, since I'm new on Yap, and I take my assets to American Express to be converted. They tell me that each of these seven-foot stone wheels are worth about seventy cents American and start to pile them on my outstretched arms. I played intramural football at Cornell, but I can't carry almost a hundred thousand dollars in millstones. My arms start to ache and the pile of coins stretches up into the sky. It really hurts and my wife says to me, "Are you sure you can handle that, Vern?" Every time I have this dream I wake up in a cold sweat with my legs aching. Once I was standing on the bathroom scale holding our extra bedding.*

This man is already reasonably successful, and so it is no surprise that his understanding of money is as keen as it is. What we notice even in this dollars-and-cents nightmare is that the issue is once again the threat of humiliation and not the acquisition of money, which would be what we would imagine an ambitious man's healthy fantasy to be. Cold cash, like the snow bricks that build an igloo, seem to be the protection against humiliation that men need to amass like bodyguards.

Dreams, in their directness, deal with life as most men fear they deserve to live it—in shame. Harnessing that apprehension has built empires (not to mention foundations). Dreams educate the individual by dangling unlikely destinies in front of him and urging him to jump in order to avoid them. And for him it's the same choice faced by a stunned doe bathed in oncoming headlights: jump or perish.

HARNESSING INNER ENERGIES, OR WHAT MAKES SAMMY JOG?

Although college football stars turn their rambunctiousness in the end to selling insurance, most executives would agree that physical exertion and getting ahead are not necessarily synonymous. Regular rounds of golf and squash do reassure potential customers (and superiors, which amounts to the same thing in this business of self-selling) that your energies are enthusiastically safe, but all you really need do is allude to such activities before sitting down to lunch early in any business flirtation.

Whatever their faults, flagpole-sitters of the 1930s at least kept to themselves and never claimed to be closer to God when they hovered above the Wrigley Building. Faddists of the last decade, however, have loudly propagandized the powers of a strict physical regimen to maximize one's deepest capabilities. This, too, can be as easily claimed as practiced, and for most of you, just reading these few paragraphs will suffice to bluff your way through discussions of self-understanding, and then you'll need think no more about it.

RUNNING. Now that yoga has progressed from the ascetic to coffee-table-book status, the floodgates of arcane exercise have been opened wide. Rushing ahead foremost among these modes is *running,* a rite that apparently satisfies our evolutionary trump card, the urge to flee. Running has been ascribed more transcendental properties than the Holy Eucharist, and its rise from oddity to banality has transfigured the urban landscape as much as the automobile has, though to less purpose. Symbolically, running prepares many for corporate life, particularly if they run on an enclosed circular track with no one watching. Runners quickly learn to expend most of their energies not in the sport itself, but in lugging home books on the subject and in explaining its edifying ways in barely patient monotones to nonpractitioners, a mystical variant of one-upmanship that even Tartuffe would admire.

There are several exercises that help tone and shape the muscles needed for self-advancement. Running by itself does foster a dull-eyed monomania that behooves the ambitious, but a little fine-detail work is also needed.

THE HELD BREATH. The respiratory gymnastics incumbent upon most yes-men would make bagpipers and swami alike run for the highlands. Some Madison Avenue back-up men are so skilled at swallowing objections along with their pride that they can keep silent for hours at a time, before even the most driveling and fatuous of superiors. To strengthen your ability to maintain job-conserving silence, stand in front of a mirror and hold your breath for an hour every day, beginning with ten-minute stretches and working up to what is called the "assistant-chief aria"—sixty solid minutes of stolid agreeability. Try Scotch-taping photos of war atrocities and professional sportscasters to a wall, and then see if you can retain your breath-holding even in contemplation of such decry-ables as these. When you've perfected the technique, you will be ripe for an advisorship to even the most powerful in your firm.

THE GRIN-FROWN.   Isometrics have enjoyed a considerable revival since the children who made all those froggy faces in the schoolyard have grown up to be physical therapists. One exercise that can benefit the rising businessperson is the combination grin-frown, a challenging contortion that requires the apparent expression of two contradictory verdicts simultaneously. This calisthenic is particularly useful in confabs with multiple- and variously-minded superiors, or in conference with a higher-up whose own desires and opinions are fuzzy or inaccessible to you.

THE SIDE STEP.   Often called "the dance of diplomats," this exercise requires a few props, such as ordinary table lamps or books, or large plush toys from the children's playroom. Strew the living room floor with these articles, adding golf balls, tacks, and even assorted free-running gerbils as your proficiency increases. Learn to circle and weave through the room, talking incessantly, without ever touching any of the obstacles as you careen around. Many policy-framers and public relations wizards have sharpened their sidestepping skills to such a point that they can tap-dance on a parquet floor without once touching a crack.
 Some readers may wonder why exercise is treated here

as a modern innovation, considering that our forebears did plenty of it, albeit not during their scheduled leisure hours. The fact is, exercise is older than even the quintessentially human trait of self-consciousness, but *self-conscious exercise* is a combo of fairly recent vintage; the barbell and the telephone rose to prominence at about the same time, as the white-collar classes began to proliferate. When the movements of the body become as considered and deliberate as those of the mind, we have an up-to-the-minute personality and, incidentally, a true Slave of Success.

THE MEDICINE CHEST
OF SUCCESS

Fortunately for tens of thousands of unnaturally zestful executives, the horse-racing practice of postcompetition urinalysis hasn't yet been adopted by the arbiters of corporate ethics. The foreign substances to be found in a blood sample from many successful men would rival those in any disqualified thoroughbred. And while we neither condemn nor condone the abuse of energizing drugs, a daily 500 mg dose of Benzedrine has more than once made the difference between a respectably earnest career and one of interminable accomplishment. Less risky and more in keeping with our recommended first-strike defensive posture is a reverse, negative application of controlled substances: Powerful sedatives gradually sluiced into the office water cooler may make for some parched afternoons as far as you're concerned, but your antagonists will be tucked into a perpetual limbo of impotent mellowness.

It's the shortsighted success-seeker who doesn't read between the lines of nutrition books (and, indeed, of every seemingly straightforward assertion he encounters) and apply that interlinear reading to practice. When the pamphlets tell you that niacin "helps prevent loss of appetite," *your* thoughts should leap immediately to those extensive business lunches you're required to grin through daily. If the vitamin A in carrots is said to be "good for the eyesight," eat bushel baskets of the precious root every day: Your vision will become acute enough to read confidential memos lying across a conference table, or private diaries sitting unattended on a neighboring desk. The caveat "Eyes Only" can become one more petty proscription for you to ignore (or reinterpret), like the Biblical strictures against covetousness and pride.

As to the more esoteric tablets and salves recommended by other success-mongers, we hesitate to offend our friends in pharmaceuticals with categorical recommendations. But we do know one chief operating officer who would sooner treat his employees as equals than forgo his daily application of placental ointment. Real estate whizzes, by and large, bathe in pollen.

In short, if you restrict your use of chemistry's bounty to aspirin and bicarb, soon all you'll have is your health. That sparkle-eyed former office boy will be clearing out your desk for the last time, and you'll be about as close to control of Wall Street as any Christian Scientist.

EXTRAS!
EXTRAS!

READ ALL
ABOUT 'EM!

---

*The road of excess leads to the
palace of wisdom.*
> —William Blake,
> "Proverbs of Hell"

A canny fellow once said: "As long as there's got to be the
proverbial carrot on a stick, you might as well make it the
biggest, juiciest carrot you can find." Whether he realized it
or not, the man was talking about perks and benefits. (They
used to be called fringe benefits until a carping sociology
graduate student observed that they were rather central to
any meaningful estimate of a man's earnings.) For salary, or
its sometimes-synonym "personal fulfillment," makes up
only half of the employee-compensation story.

    And speaking of impressive roots, it's the rare cor-
porate climber who knows (or has the wherewithal to know)
the full Latin root of the slang phrase "perk," as in, "Hey,
Bob, you know that load of medicine and foodstuffs that
was supposed to go to the Peruvian refugees? Well, the boss

---

said I could have it all—as a *perk*." This favored diminutive of "perquisite" is as smart and jaunty as the stockbroker at the country club buffet; "perk" makes stolen staplers and leased Impalas sound downright wholesome. If you remember your schoolboy Latin, you know that perquisite derives from the verb *perquirere,* "to search for." Whether it's the *search for* wisdom and meaning or our modern *search for* tax-free heaps of expensive gin and the finest beef, perquisites speak to a need as basic as food, shelter, and the marvelous new *textures* in resort wear for men.

Just what is a perquisite? It is not, like "happiness" or "success," an easily defined and universally understood commodity. Perks come in myriad sizes, shapes, and saliences, from the free rags given your troop of office cleaning women to the unlimited bonhomie provided by most advertising agencies. It's important for you to be able to distinguish a perquisite from a mere booby prize, a benefit from a table scrap, a junket from a fool's errand, a pliant, unthreatening man from a man who merely likes you.

Perks have had a lot of bad press recently. Not long ago, for instance, there were rumors afly about the international aerospace concern that was maintaining litters of puppies in posh East Side apartments for Japanese businessmen to play with and pet. Maybe so. But who did it hurt?

Not fifty years ago, even major corporations could get by with offering perks no more alluring than free home-safety tips and unlimited access to the company's recipe file. For some living (but forcibly retired) executives, the loot of today's perquisites was once a preposterous fantasy. Businesspeople bought their own meals, and no employee expected his firm to finance a clumsy child's dislocated shoulder. Back then, the perks and benefits were ephemeral bordering on invisible. Yet unbeknownst to most contemporary corporate cogs, these scores of old-time perks *exist still*. Appreciating them simply requires a new attitude toward self-consolation, a new sensitivity to the:

FORGOTTEN PERQUISITES

They may not possess the cachet of three-week fact-finding trips to Aruba and company-supplied concubines, but without the Forgotten Perquisites, we all might be a lot closer to rabblehood. Notable among these is the chief perk of omission, that is, Not Having Your Name Embroidered Over Your Shirt ·Pocket. In some parts of the country, where obliquity is less prized, this perquisite is simply called Not Being a Uniformed Manual Laborer. But whatever you call it, it means the same thing: you may detest your job making check marks and initialing scratch paper, but nobody ever asks you for a handcart or an oily rag, and you are presumed not to have a wrench on your person. Forgotten Perquisites abound, of course—there's On-the-Job Freedom of Thought, for instance—and luxuriating in their very commonness is tantamount to (or at least a simulacrum of) actually bettering your lot. Forgotten perks though they may be, only a saint or a fool takes *anything* for granted in the office miasma, least of all his basic human due.

That was the past, before O.S.H.A., before Tongsun Park. Today, of course, perks encompass any sort of company-provided luxury, with an emphasis on those that cater to kinky weaknesses. Virtually anything fun that the I.R.S. can't prove *isn't* a business expense can be a perk. Today you want *things,* and you want them pronto.

OFFICE SUPPLIES

The degree of your physical detachment from actual production—from terrific heat and rhythmic cacophony and heavy-duty matériel—is a fair measure of the success of your plan for success. Odds are that yours is an occupation so tediously rarefied and superfluous that your grandparents would have found it baffling, if not reprehensible: You work in an office, that's all you really know, distant from the clang and fire, and the verbs on your résumé tend toward "coordinate," "facilitated," "presented," and, in a few exceptional cases, "conceived."

The spoils open to your petty plundering in the office constitute only a mean subsistence. Yellow legal pads, thumbtacks, carbon paper, and even fancy felt-tip pens can only satisfy one's desperate remunerative lusts for a while. It's true, for a year—perhaps two—otherwise unremarkable evening homecomings are transformed by breathless squeals of excitement. "*Look,* honey! Look at all these great rubber bands I got for *free* at the office today!" But sooner than you might think, the glee grows rote. Even wholly unfettered office thievery eventually palls. "Here—it's another gross of rubber-stamp ink pads. Take them and put them with the rest, or, well, you know . . . whatever you want to do." The disappointment (a mild form of what highly paid consultants call Embezzler's Malaise) can be forestalled if you are the parent of young children. Typewriter ribbons become beloved playthings for inventive tots, and manila folders are always good sport for any child with a healthy urge for logical organization. But in the long run, even an infinite supply of "Par Avion" envelopes is not a satisfactory substitute for plenty of first-class trips on actual *avions* themselves.

MEDICAL INSURANCE

Having someone else spring for your ulcer treatments is surely a more significant privilege than free Xerox copies. But employee insurance is nothing to brag about; it has now become such a commonplace that it is a benefit enjoyed by clerical staffers, blue-collar workers, and even some fresh-water fishes. But *the occasions on which you use* your insurance privileges may be crucial checkpoints on your precarious chase down the autobahn to success. Most employers monitor closely their underlings' Blue Cross dossiers; in some particularly democratic firms, a summary of each employee's physical condition is regularly posted in the company lunchroom. A publicized predisposition to angina might be enough to make your superiors think twice about granting you the transfer to that high-pressure arbitrage project. Some customarily private little cancer of the bowels could nix your chances for any position requiring prolonged client contact; incontinence is never attractive, and certainly not desirable during a daylong negotiating session with federal regulators. Any affliction even vaguely connected with sexual (or human) contact will irreparably tarnish an employee's record, nor will it do to be treated for any disease traditionally the subject of old wives' tales.

The simple solution is to restrict use of your company-paid medical insurance to cases where the injury or infirmity will materially *improve* your standing in the eyes of senior management. Sprains and simple fractures are excellent, especially when they might have been incurred on the playing fields, but a shattered fibula is overdoing it .and a pulled muscle too redolent of coy understatement. Benign tumors—skin cancer is good—give you an air of maturity and resolve.

Conversely, earaches, broken noses, and even the flu can make you seem childish, and it is always unwise to submit claims for cases of swallowed Silly Putty or one's penis stuck in a pants zipper. Periodic reimbursements for routine surgical procedures are generally appropriate: modern medicine's discreet appendectomy scars, for example, grant you an unspoken macho snarl in the steam room, and even the hideous pain of kidney stones has its compensations in that affliction's gritty, no-nonsense, heavy-industry overtones.

If major surgery is absolutely necessary, an artificial organ can be just the thing to convince the boss that your innards are nonpareil in state-of-the-art high technology, a walking piece of R. & D. On the other hand, treatments involving herbal poultices and laudanum elixirs can make you appear backward and out of step.

Finally, except in the limited-time-frame world of corporate consulting, it is better to leave terminal diseases untreated than to raise the risk of a premature career downturn. A lame duck is so called only when his chronic gimp is known. Keep mum and die successful.

EDUCATIONAL BENEFITS

Some meretriciously good-natured companies will reimburse employees for tuition expenses related to the worker's piecemeal attempts at self-improvement. The same caveats that obtained for medical insurance apply here: your bosses will have no difficulty learning exactly what subjects you've been studying and the grades received. A transcript filled with courses like "Macaroni Handicrafts," "Videotaping Your Lawn," and "Profits Are for Suckers" can raise doubts about your intellectual mettle, and indeed your very human worth. The only entirely safe courses are those with which you already have some familiarity. A carefully concealed undergraduate *summa* in medieval architecture, for example, should ensure high marks in night school's Med. Arch. 203. Superiors will be impressed by your extravocational brilliance, and if you happen to be in the business of selling mammoth stone gargoyles, so much the better.

Increasingly common are companies that send off promising but meagerly credentialed managers to proper graduate business schools. There they are given remedial training in skills such as input-output analysis, survey research, nonverbal communication, and overweening self-confidence. This second type of educational boondoggle entails no serious downside risks, apart from the indenture with which you and your firstborn son are legally obliged afterward.

TRANSPORTATION

Free laminated city bus schedules are not the sort of thing we have in mind. Even discounted subway tokens and ample space for bicycle storage ought not to quench your perk-lust in this connection. Plush Lear jets shared with strong, silver-haired men you wish your father had looked like; enormous limousines for trips of only a few blocks; frequent commercial airline travel to randomly chosen, far-away Sunbelt cities; at the very least a brand-new energy-inefficient car for your exclusive use, and with no unseemly slogans or telephone numbers stenciled on the doors. Mobility is one of your most profoundly desired goals. Why not begin in this narrowly literal realm and travel in style, or at least incessantly?

EXPENSE-ACCOUNT MEALS

Now we're talking significant incentives to give up those dreams of a quiet little life in custom boot making, better even than the onus of parental disapproval. Vague populist badinage has made us all aware of the "three-martini lunch." But the typical worker of the world (for whom "the good old days" connote hunting, gathering, and not walking erect) knows mercifully little about the magic and magnitude of the modern American expense account. The expense account is an institution publicly shrugged off by its fortunate devotees, explained away as a mundane fact of white-collared life. But the account executives and magazine editors and compliance officers clearly have, like the pre-Columbian priesthoods with their sacrificial slaughters, a deeply vested interest in downplaying the glamour of their prerogatives. In fact, the expense account is a nearly unlimited license to live the expansive life, if not the good one.

LUNCHES

Enormous, splendid meals taken in palacelike unction parlors, lunches are the expense-account flagship. Not only are you directly granted thousands of dollars worth of rich, glistening food, but your (carefully selected) luncheon companions are subsequently obliged to reciprocate with equal or greater largesse. As a result, in a few of our larger cities the universal expense account has made possible extraordinary "chain lunches," with some early chain participants ultimately enjoying *years* of free lunches, albeit in the company of complete strangers, many of whom speak only Portuguese.

There are expense-account dinners as well, naturally, and it is as important as it is difficult to keep away neglected spouses from the after-dark trough. Not only can spouses (and children, and mothers) interfere with the dubious business at hand during a working dinner, but the benefits of reciprocity do not apply. And you'll quickly find that the presence of wives can confuse and even offend the better class of call girl (she, too, an expense-account item).

Liquor is a prominent (and, as ever, telling) factor in the expense-account equation. If charges for hard liquor do not appear regularly on your expense-account vouchers, certain unflattering notations will be made in your permanent file. Alcoholic entertainment is valued above all for its unequaled cost-efficiency: five drinks of premium liquor cost your treasury no more than a mediocre lunch for one person, and under certain circumstances—just before sensitive labor contract talks, for instance—the dividends can be enormous for the dedicated host.

So, you're out to lunch with the boss and an important customer at some swank spot where they serve steak five inches thick. What *type* of liquor should you order if you've more on your mind than relaxation? Martinis are acceptable but trite, while any standard whiskey is properly robust, although rye or one of the Canadian blends might suggest a certain gratuitous individualism. The preferred suffix for whiskey orders is "and water," soda being just slightly effeminate, or Continental, or both. Whiskey, especially bourbon, should never be ordered "straight up"—without ice or water—lest your fellow drinkers think you a rube or a lush, the sole exception being at industrial sales conferences, where the participants—rubes or lushes, every one of them—will be insensible of any stylistic faux 'pas on your part.

If you travel in the course of your work, learn about

regional peculiarities. Scotch-and-Ovaltines, for instance, are not commonly ordered in New England. Nasal-spray-and-tonics are sold only by the drink in several Midwestern states, and in Minnesota sparkling wines are never properly served with (or to) fowl. Ordering "a big Shirley Temple with lots and lots of ice, pretty please" will simply not do outside of certain coastal enclaves, and any request for aperitifs will be construed in Arkansas as veiled sexual suggestion by all but the most sophisticated businessmen.

HOTELS

Most successful men actually prefer hotel rooms to their own homes, even those with wives skilled at fashioning paper sanitary rings and whittling down soap bars. There is nothing like a suite at a Hyatt Regency for finally making sense out of all the pain, the struggle, the nagging sense of spiritual void: clean as a whistle, all smoked-glass sleekness and plaid order, and all charged off to the company. Some salesmen, journalists, and vaudevillians claim to weary of "life on the road," with its successive nights of hotel beds and restaurant food. But a man who claims to dislike staying in a good hotel room is a man ill suited to life at the top; sleeping in a crisp bed in some anonymous room without a single caterwauling loved one nearby, this is a rare privilege, not a rigor.

CLUBS

We don't mean an unused toolshed behind your best friend's house that you've painted purple. We don't mean some fraternal order whose members specialize in public self-humiliation and charitable skin grafts. A company-paid club membership is a reliable mark of corporate success. If you are a likely candidate for this particular (and particularly excessive) perk, you already know it, and you've been stocking up on white shoe polish and smutty stories for years. If not, no amount of advice from us will confer on you that self-assured shimmer of clubability. If you should, somehow, win admission to some exclusive sanctum or other, two words of warning: first, you'd best temper that old habit of scrupulous candor about your ancestry; and second, ordering magnums of champagne and huge platters of oysters Rockefeller at every meal will generally not be taken as evidence of your aristocratic mien.

STOCK OPTIONS

Buy low, sell high, and don't brag to anyone who looks like an employee of the Securities and Exchange Commission.

A MISCELLANEOUS PRESENT,
A MIRACULOUS FUTURE

The world of perquisites and that of ethics needn't meet, or even glance at each other across a crowded room. The corporate cornucopia's apex is dark and shadowy, and there lurk invitingly all the no-interest loans, the free legal advice, the endless investment counsel, and the convenient packets of cold cash in various amounts on various pretexts. Everybody knows stories of a vice-president's dining room freshly remodeled on the whispered orders of some accommodating shop steward, and the simple corner office is a fiercely coveted prize for which many businesspeople are willing (and even eager) to sacrifice their friendships, their families, all food and drink for a year, and eternal salvation.

But the upwardly grappling mob becomes accustomed and even jaded to the conventional perquisites. Cuisinart insurance is one popular new perk among middle-level marketing executives, as is a year's supply of the correct wines with complete instructions on how and when to serve them. For employees in hardship posts, corporate paternalism spares no expense. The executive transferred abroad can count on receiving sympathetic media coverage, survivors' insurance for the family, as well as Berlitz-style courses in basic commands to the guard dogs of his host nation. Several Chicago firms now retain inhouse blues bands that specialize in treating employees who wish to refurbish their mojos or to ease their worried minds.

Yet for many senior executives, clubs, daily limousines, immense profit sharing, and all the rest are not enough to regenerate flagging commitment. A few especially powerful multinational companies, desperate to attract and keep the very finest managerial talent, now offer inducements such as food tasters and jesters on twenty-four-hour call, posthumously awarded Congressional Medals of Honor for all of one's English-speaking ancestors, and full voting membership in the Soviet Politburo.

More probably sooner than later, though, no treasure trove of mere gifts will satisfy the venal men and women at the very pinnacle of achievement and reward. For the chief executive who has literally every*thing,* one well-known consulting firm has devised and will shortly begin recommending a novel—and perhaps ultimate—employment benefit. Tentatively called Metaperk, the plan calls for companies to offer a written, legally enforceable "Guarantee of Happiness." It remains unclear what might be the specific judicial

remedies for a wronged executive under Metaperk (mone-
tary damages? effusive apologies?) aside from an unassail-
able sense of righteousness vis à vis one's employer. Yet
that, in the end, may be the most satisfying perquisite of
all.

YOU'VE COME A LONG WAY,

> *A whore is a woman who sells only her body for money.*
> —Robert Musil

In the best of all possible worlds there would be no need for this chapter. A book about people stepping on other people would be understood to apply equally to all, regardless of sex, race, creed, or family ties. But we would be shirking our responsibility if we were to confuse this pretty utopian vision with the cruel reality. The hard fact is that if you are a woman with ambition in a corporation today, you are a fish out of water swimming upstream. Accordingly, we dedicate this chapter to you.

Nevertheless, we encourage men to read this chapter carefully. Many male Success Clinic graduates report that their lives were forever changed by our discussion of the plight of the managerial woman, that it opened their eyes to the bias and humiliation their sisters are up against, and that it gave them a deeper understanding of themselves. (But if it's getting late and you've already passed New Canaan station, you'd better skip straight ahead to page 75. Also, try not to move your lips when you read; it isn't that the practice makes you appear dim [though it does], but that *others* might then read your lips and steal the valuable secrets intended for you alone.)

People often ask: "Where do three little t—— who've never done a lick of work in their lives get off writing about the predicament of the working woman today?" When we're asked this to our faces, we point out that we've listened intensively to hundreds of women pour out their frustrations, their horror stories, their hang-ups, and their thwarted aspirations. Frankly, one of us cried, although now he won't admit it. We listened to some long, heartrending, shocking tales in some crowded, hoity-toity restaurants with guess-who picking up the tabs. (Even when they "pay for themselves" they leave out tax and tip.) But as these ladies shared moments from their lives, we found that an interesting thing happened. We found that our minds were opened, our lives were touched, and we grew. And, in time, we grew so much that eventually we were able to help women to grow too, much better than they'd ever be able to do on their own.

Power games come naturally to men. No sooner have two mothers complimented each other on the new "character" lent each other by nascent crow's-feet and stray silver hairs, than their young male charges have vanished out the back door to vie for the tallest, fastest, strongest, longest, and all the other superlatives that are the laureates of their age. They are displaying a competitiveness that will very likely never slacken but merely be turned to new accounts.

Women, on the other hand, tend to stay aloof from all this. Perhaps they are offended by the aggression, the boasting, the noise, and the animalism, or maybe they are simply bored by it all. They nod knowingly to each other and wait demurely on the sidelines until the boys have had their fill of these often cruel, always silly puerile stunts, and then the girls give themselves sexually to the winner.

Thus, having seen themselves for so long as a trophy, a prize, a chattel, many women have difficulty entering the arena in their new role as gladiatrix. For men, the what's-behind-the-curtain-Carol of life was *Carol*—and Anne and Barbara and Jennifer. But what will be the prize for women? Certainly not the approval of men. Self-respect? Dignity? A sense of independence and human worth? Pretty abstract when it's time to turn out the lamp and try to go to sleep. And if it's hard now, imagine it when you're old, infirm, a burden to your "friend," and Carson's been off the air for decades.

There was a time when men considered power to be their exclusive birthright, a responsibility that they are innately better qualified than women to assume. But the twentieth century has changed all that. Archaeologists have unearthed evidence of primitive societies in which women held all the positions of political and priestly authority, while men stayed at home puttering around the cliff dwelling, trading cassava recipes, and buggering the children. Several *Star Trek* episodes documented entire planets ruled by women. And the Greek poetess Sappho is believed to have been a woman. The eminent sociologist Max Judenfrage has observed that "if man's more robust physique ever had justified his dominance in the workplace, the preeminence of the white-collar bureaucrat in today's postindustrial society makes such an excuse ludicrous today." Professor Judenfrage, arguably a homosexual, goes on to point out that new scientific techniques of aptitude testing have demonstrated conclusively that women actually score higher than male peers in guessing the antonyms of obsolescent words, select-ing the best titles for paragraphs about new advancements in chemical glassware, and in following directions generally.

Over the last century, the American woman has made great strides in demanding and attaining her political and legal rights and her social liberation. But there can be no doubt that in the America of the 1980s the working woman's battle for power and financial success remains a long, thankless uphill venture. We wouldn't even try it if we were you, especially if you're half-decent looking.

Many men are unaware of how their habitual acts of what they term "chivalry" or "simple courtesy" may serve to subordinate women colleagues and superiors. The woman executive's workday must therefore be an eight-hour vigil in which she inspects men's every careless and contradictory gesture for its deep-rooted meaning, just as the wary scholar delves into conflicting ancient chronicles searching for the underlying dissertation topic.

We were present at a board meeting once during which a woman vice-president was delivering a competent and busi-nesslike presentation of quarterly earnings figures for chro-mium tennis ball repressurizers, when the president of the company, a political liberal with a reputation for openminded fairness, decided to break for lunch. Without thinking, however, he called over his vice-president and whis-pered to her, "It's Harold's fiftieth birthday and we bought him a big cake. Cora, would you be a dear and leap out of the cake nude for us?" Afraid of hurting her boss's feelings over an obviously isolated request, she made a serious tac-tical error and did as she was bid. In fairness to her, later on in the lunch she did draw the line and refuse to copulate with a circus pony brought in for the festivities. But the damage had already been done. When she resumed her presentation after the party, with icing still peeking out around the ears, male executives refused to take her seriously, despite her admirable cogency and sober demeanor.

Men's sexism is so early inculcated and so deeply ingrained that almost any overt femininity is likely to be associated in their minds with their tawdry secretaries and concubines. Most successful women have hit upon some formula for dressing smartly and attractively, while conjuring up neither the lesbian* image on the one hand, nor that of the Whore of Babylon on the other. The examples of Carrie Nation and Rosa Luxemburg, of course, leap to mind—and theirs should be studied carefully—but there have probably been others.

The managerial woman has confidence in her own dignity and competence as a person, confidence that allows her to enjoy her own sexuality without relying on it. Your clothes announce to the world that you are proud of being a successful, powerful person in your own right, but that you are also proud of being a woman.

But how to achieve that look?

The tweed skirt and jacket are, by now, fashion cliché. It looked fine on Joan Crawford and Rosalind Russell, but you happen to fall a little closer to the edge of the spectrum that produces Aeroflot stewardesses and small toolsheds, so learn to accept who you are and begin the task of trying to hide it.

You're looking for a businesslike womanhood that doesn't shout its identity—a playfully ascetic style we call the "un-dress." Your dress should communicate its message without drawing attention to itself. In short, strive to achieve the aura of a bulletin board.

---

* Not that there's anything wrong with being a lesbian. Most managerial women are.

Admittedly, these are trying times for those who would go around in fashion circles. When trend-setters are wearing off-the-shoulder gowns with flak jackets and bowling shoes, the working woman may begin to lose her bearings. Designer-name clothes, if you can afford them, guarantee a toehold on decorum amid this treacherous chaos. Ralph Lauren and Calvin Klein have proven helpful to many managerial women willing to forgo food, and at least one of our huskier lady friends has had some charming work done for her by Christo. Some daring women even get away with wearing designer blue jeans to the workplace, though they must arrange to be seen by colleagues only from the rear and while resting all of their weight on their right thighs. But one must never get carried away by what looks good in a magazine—as those many of you in the advertising business are indifferently aware. What fits and suits Lauren Hutton can cause the bends in a woman of more quotidian dimension.

If designer clothes seem out of your league, there is another easy, if poorly understood, path to tastefulness. It happens that a certain outfit—first isolated by Sir John Priestly in the eighteenth century, who called it "the Natural ensemble"—will universally trigger the response "Oh, how tasteful!" in all sane adult human beings the world over. It consists of a dark skirt and dark boots meeting just below the knee, topped with a beige cashmere pullover sweater. No one really knows why this is so.

As an alternative to the natural ensemble, however, one of us is especially fond of the combination of a white tank top tucked into glossy red jogging shorts worn with three-inch spike heels. The other two of us kind of go for those things certain girls wear with only one strap over the right shoulder that wind across the torso like the cheetah hide Tarzan's Jane used to wear. Or how about those dresses that aren't really see-through, but maybe just barely, and that unbutton way up the side, so tight on lean flanks that with high heels the girl's feet just click-click-click like little pistons in a modified goose step across the floor.

The correct accessories can lend just the right touch of wit and sportiveness to otherwise conservative office attire. An Italian silk scarf is a sophisticated but feminine tie substitute (see Friedrich Hauptmann's *Tie Envy in Women*, 1951). And by all means wear jewelry. We advise delicate minimalist Danish bracelets or slender gold necklaces, but not the pendulous chandelier earrings stolen for you by an old boyfriend named "Sunshine."

With respect to undergarments, the managerial woman has a bit more flexibility, although it is probably a good idea to steer clear of anything involving whalebone or sophisticated architectural principles.

The managerial woman must view her life as an incessant caulking of the myriad leaks through which her latent femininity threatens to seep out into visibility. She must eschew cutesy nicknames like "Cricket" or "Butter." She must never begin memos with little epigrams lifted from Joni Mitchell lyrics and should refrain from changing the dots over *i*'s to big, fat flowers. Letters should close with a simple "Sincerely" or "Sincerely yours," not "Luv ya," and should be typed on standard corporation letterhead bond, not on scented Peanuts stationery. If there happen to be two managerial women in one corporation, they should never pass notes, whisper secrets in front of others, or speak French if they are not French.

Of course, not every manifestation of vestigial femininity must be mercilessly squelched. In fact, some cunning women have learned to use the symbols of their sex to lure and throw men off balance, to use their manhood against them with the adroitness of a judo black belt. Remember that anything a woman does that a man doesn't do takes on the quality of a secondary sexual characteristic: switching from street boots to more comfy office pumps; using words like "comfy" and "pumps"; dieting; intoning declarative sentences so that they curl up at the end like a question; feigning cramps; reading huge James Michener novels all the way through in a day and a half. These constitute the essence of womanhood to a man.

The managerial woman's office is her home turf, and she can make of that territory a feminine game preserve where the endangered fauna and flora of the female biosphere are permitted to run wild, transforming her neutral little cubicle into an emotional minefield for any male subordinate unfortunate enough to venture in. One savvy woman director of public relations we know hangs five or six pairs of nylons on venetian blinds, lamps, and coatracks, suffusing the room with a pungent, synthetic, female-but-unfeminine ambience. A diaphragm is draped nonchalantly over a paperweight on one of the ironing boards she uses in lieu of a desk. At staff conferences her tall backless stool is the only other furniture, obliging all her male employees to kneel or sit "Indian Fashion" on the cool, dusty linoleum floor before her. More than one nonplussed male exec has been halted in the middle of a sales report by the director's feared imperative, "Hold still," followed by her solicitous plucking of a stray white thread from his Brooks Brothers three-piece.

Just as she booby-traps her office with the squeamish male in mind, she peppers her speech with off-the-cuff references to women's gamier processes: "I was out at the water cooler this morning menstruating, when suddenly it occurred to me . . ." After one particularly grueling digression involving pessaries, we witnessed a World War II vet, decorated for valor in the Pacific theater, back out of the room, gagging and pitiably extending a crucifix between himself and his petite tormentress.

Yes, it's an exciting time to be a woman. There is no greater excitement than work itself—the chance to dress up *every* day, to earn your own pin money, to meet dynamic men with really great personalities.

Over the last century, the American woman has made great strides in demanding and attaining her political and legal rights and her social liberation. When Henrik Ibsen dared to depict Nora walking out on her husband and child almost a century ago, he could never have dreamed that one day secretaries would go to work in pantsuits and refuse to make coffee for their bosses.

PROFILES IN

M⬤⬤LAH

ALDEN SHORTFORD
PETTYPOINT

Yes, I think I'm pretty important.
But after I'm gone, someone else
will come along who thinks he's
pretty important, so my work will
be carried on.
—Alden Shortford Pettypoint

When Alden Shortford Pettypoint died, on May 3, 1977, the
New York Transportation Authority paid tribute to him by
running all trains on time for a period of twelve hours. To
observe mourning, the National Telephone and Telegraph
System discontinued connecting all but its own calls for the
next three days. Schoolchildren recited his name at as-
semblies, and Congress approved a farewell letter to him
that is currently on display in the Library of Congress, since
no one knew where to mail it.

Who was this man, that tycoons and tykes, that high-
brows and hoboes alike felt his passing, as of a wind,

sweeping across the country with a democratic malodor? And who, if any, knew him well?

In many ways he was a man of contradictions, and in many ways he wasn't. His chief aide for years, Byron Wheeler, summed up his late employer in these words: "You're trying to trick me into saying something *crazy,* aren't you? I know how you guys operate. Get me to let something *wild* slip, you get it into the headlines, and pretty soon it's the class geek who gets stuck playing me in the school Current Events Pageant. No thanks, Mister Muckraking Journalism! Infamy I don't need. What was he like? Like a human being! There's human interest for you!"

This does little to dispel the clouds of mystery that surround Pettypoint and have, according to meteorologists, since 1946. Even the Pettypoint Gallery, a collection of his acquired paintings and statuary, has a Fifth Avenue address that no one has ever successfully located, though photographs of its exterior occasionally surface in Japanese tourist magazines. The millionaire seemed to thrive on such secrecy, and would not even participate in knock-knock jokes because it involved answering too many questions. His personal valet never spoke to him except via walkie-talkie, and his own parents are fuzzy about the circumstances of his birth.

As near as research can determine, however, Alden Shortford Cogbinder Pettypoint was born of nameless and faceless immigrants on New York's Lower East Side. (Perhaps it is the disadvantage of facelessness that makes it so difficult for his parents even now to discuss him.) His patrician name bespeaks no Brahmin background, for it is a composite of four of the largest garment sweatshops in the neighborhood at the time of his birth. This curious patronymic style was less felicitously expressed in his younger sister's name, Nathan Nedick Crosstown-Bus-Stop. The year of Alden's birth is unknown, but he was still being carded in bars as late as 1919, so the date is conceded to be about 1895. The day is unknown, but Pettypoint, a lover of symmetry, always celebrated his birthday on May 3, since it was also the day on which he died.

The Pettypoint household was neither gracious nor small; in addition to the nameless, faceless parents was a faceless sister, a brother who was nameless, although he did have a face, and a chauffeur who, although lacking an automobile, had ample face and several names, the latter owing to a previous career outside the law. Despite its bid for elegance (the chauffeur carried visitors piggyback up and down the stairs of the five-flight walk-up), the family was ragged, and one of them, though it's not clear which, didn't smell very good. Alden's mother had dreams of gentility and refinement stemming from her once having looked at stereopticon pictures of faraway places. She taught him to smoke cigarettes at an early age, in the hope that his stunted growth would relieve the expense of new clothes. She was frail and birdlike, and spoke alternately in a southern and Irish accent. From her, Alden inherited an artistic spirit and a great love for her.

All that is known of Alden's father is that he spent many years as an immigrant laborer in the garment district, and that he was the secretary of state under William Howard Taft. Beyond that, all is mere conjecture, though much of the conjecture is juicy and fascinating. In his memoirs (*None of Your Goddamn Business,* Viking Press, 1972) Pettypoint does not mention his father and, indeed, mentions very little else. It is assumed this relationship with his father was quite painful, since it is not human nature to spare listeners the merely dull.

When it came time for the eldest son to be sent to school, Alden's parents debated entrusting him to either Andover or Exeter, but finally settled on selling him to a children's workhouse closer to home. This proved too much for Alden, and he ran away for good at age ten, taking only forged documents proving he was an orphan. Twelve blocks uptown, he traded his papers for a shovel and got a job digging basements for skyscrapers, which were just then coming into vogue. At night, he added to his meager earnings by hawking used matches outside the opera house. Both jobs were exhausting and brought little remuneration, but young Alden, evincing a flair for the autobiographical that portended his eventual fame, stuck to the employment for over a year, comforted by the prospect of recounting his future past hardships.

One night in 1907, winter, the ersatz orphan was offering his preburned matches to sympathetic but resistant first-nighters at a production of *Aïda*. Snow had fallen and a parked carriage near the stage door was skirted with snow. Since Alden traveled everywhere with his shovel (he slept under it and used it to fry eggs over fires), he was enlisted to help clear the carriage wheels. After some digging, the notion was hit upon to use Alden as a wedge to free the ice-bound wheels. His stunted size served the task well, and the carriage owner, Rhinestone Rob Grady, offered Alden a permanent position on his company staff. Alden accepted.

Rhinestone Rob Grady was famous for his extravagant fur coats, his liberal gifts to beautiful women, and his fondness for overeating to the point of losing consciousness. He had made his money through profiteering, whatever that is, and by buying up all the air the railroads would have to pass through after everyone else had bought up the land itself. Whether he saw the young Pettypoint's potential is unknown, but he always referred to his young ward as "a damn fine wedge."

Alden moved into Grady's bachelor mansion, a rambling structure on Madison, Park, and part of Fifth Avenue. He was given a bath (this is where Part One of his memoirs ends) and a new shovel. He was sent on errands when there wasn't much work for him under the wheels, and he became a favorite of Rob's tenants, who, according to a Grady press release of the period, looked forward to rent day because "little Alden" was coming to collect.

Pettypoint departed from Grady in 1922 to set up his own business, the venture that would culminate four decades later in the Pettypoint Plaza in Chicago and its thousands of branch offices here and abroad. The novice businessman organized a firm that offered Orphan's Insurance, a kind of protection children could purchase to provide for themselves in the event of the sudden and untimely deaths of those who provided for them. With a few friends, Pettypoint toured local schoolyards, outlining the virtues of Orphan's Insurance to attentive recess crowds. Eventually he added a mobile slide show that graphically illustrated the sort of deaths that parents, especially careless or overtalkative parents, met every day.

Student involvement was great, and Juniors Security (his name for the insurance) skyrocketed. In later years, Pettypoint was to explain his motivation thus: "I was virtually an orphan. Naturally I was moved by the plight of orphans, and felt all children should be as well. Personal interest, of course, enlivens anyone's sympathy."

The stock market crash ruined many businesses and certainly put the damper on Thanksgiving in 1929. Economist Frederick R. Newman has described the Depression as an era when "a bunch of guys were spending money they didn't, you know, *have* and stuff." Pettypoint's business, though shaken by the crash, survived it, and Pettypoint even collected half a million dollars in damages by suing the Federal Reserve Bank for mental cruelty. The nation's orphanages swelled, but without adult guidance, no insured child had the legal know-how to collect from Pettypoint on his or her lost parents. Little Orphan Annie and Superman both made parentlessness seem fashionable, and more young people than ever bought coverage pending their possible waifdom.

Pettypoint himself, however, was increasingly dissatisfied with his venture. He complained that children were "immature" and announced he was seeking a business venture aimed at adults. He was forced to compromise, though, and organized an insurance foundation for actors. This move took him to Hollywood, where he began to produce films with Preston von Piston, an acclaimed German director who had come to Los Angeles in 1930 to get oranges for a party but stayed to direct a talkie biography of Beethoven called *Doctor Music*. The first movie Pettypoint produced for von Piston was a World War I flying epic called (at von Piston's insistence) *Wings, But Not Bird Wings, Man Wings*. Final title selection was an artistic luxury Pettypoint allowed von Piston, a privilege the director enjoyed to the disadvantage of their next two collaborations, *Big Train Puffing Smoke Out* and *Woman Who Pretty*.

Though some critics admired von Piston (James Agee praised his ability to hold a dollar in pennies in his mouth), his films were not commercial successes. The final movie Pettypoint produced was about a romance in a theater closed for repairs, and he himself chose the title *This Theater Is Closed for Repairs*. Again, customers seemed compelled to stay away. Pettypoint's Hollywood sojourn was not glorious.

It was in Hollywood, however, that he met his wife, the actress and socialite Kitty Veneer. Kitty (whose real name was Doggy) had been considered to play the Air Force nurse in *Wings, But Not Bird Wings, Man Wings,* but lost her chance when von Piston decided "women on the set were too distracting" and had all the female roles rendered through special effects. Pettypoint met her at a premiere party and playfully offered her money to sleep with him, and the romance was born. After a brief courtship (they went out to buy more ice) the two became man and wife, Pettypoint assuming the former role.

Kitty retired from the screen tests, and the couple moved to New York, where she began to develop her famous collection of classical and Renaissance sculpture that looked like her. Pettypoint returned to Juniors Security briefly, while planning his next move. He was a wealthy man at this time, but not yet wealthy beyond your wildest dreams.

He made several shrewd investments in 1939, most notably in vibrators, anticipating the World War II domestic market. He bought a controlling interest in an adult insurance company and a used-car lot full of old Packards. This last purchase was to promote the greatest business innovation of his career, Motorists Mutual.

He hired several hundred skilled lawyers to drive the autos cross-country, causing accidents involving his own customers along the way. The lawyers made it look like the customers' fault, collected for it, and Motorists Mutual got back every premium it paid. Pettypoint was able by this ploy to raise the rates on customers who were proving "bad risks." And by bloating existing accident statistics, Pettypoint could justify generally higher rates for all his customers.

His success led him to expand the venture: thousands of Pettypoint-appointed old ladies were sent nationwide to fall on the sidewalks or trip in the businesses of those insured by him. To supplement the network of roaming cars and old ladies, Mrs. Pettypoint trained a staff of young women who would go out and find eligible men, marry them, divorce them, collect alimony, and split the take with the firm.

By 1950 Pettypoint was so well-to-do that Ripley's *Believe It or Not* ran several installments devoted exclusively to listing all the zeroes before the decimal point in his bank account. Cole Porter alluded to him in his lyrics:

> Buy me a house, mon cher,
> A little pied-à-terre would be great.
> Something like the John Paul Getty joint
> Or the Pettypoint estate.

He was photographed in a bank vault for the cover of *Life*. Bob Hope told jokes about him. Kitty Pettypoint appeared regularly on the Ten Most Dressed List. Milton Berle told Bob Hope's jokes about him. It was at this time that Pettypoint had his nervous breakdown.

He and his wife as yet had no family, because Pettypoint was trying to figure out a way to have children, die, leave them their inheritance, and then somehow get it back. The couple did have a small staff that was kept blindfolded at all times so they would not be tempted to steal the valuable objects that decorated their home. Up to this time, though, he had displayed none of the secretiveness or eccentricities that would make him a national fascination in the sixties and seventies. He had not yet begun to speak only the first letter of the word he was thinking. He had not yet had his dogs arrested for conspiracy to evolve.

The first time that there was any mental irregularity in the Sultan of Swag (as *Time* magazine called him) was at a board meeting of Motorists Mutual in early 1953. In the middle of a discussion of potential expansion into maritime mishaps, Pettypoint asked his employees to remove their faces and show him their brains. Pettypoint repeated his request, and after a brief silence the uncomfortable staff began tugging at their faces as if to unbutton them. Following some spirited grunts and some bravura staging (one particularly ambitious junior partner closed a window on his head to suggest he would uncork it), Pettypoint's underlings looked to him again, hoping this simulation would satisfy him. Their employer surveyed them with disgust and muttered, "You didn't really try."

Alerted that their superior was entertaining crotchets, his workers expressed their alarm by being more sycophantic and agreeable than ever. The following week, Pettypoint directed his public relations staff to attend all press conferences henceforward dressed as friendly automobiles with long-lashed headlights. The costumes were designed and built, but were used only once, at the Chicago Hilton press reception during which the tycoon had his initial collapse, or as his wife called it, "round one with the booby hatch."

Surrounded by his heavily disguised P.R. people (an errant hotel detective had ticketed most of them for parking violations), he addressed a large body of reporters who had come to eat his lunch and suspect his motives. After some apparently harmless introductory remarks about how American Indians didn't have to shave and how ancient a beast the opossum is, Pettypoint's comments became unusual and disjointed. First, he divided the assembly into halves and attempted to direct them in a contrapuntal version of "Roll Me Over in the Clover." The reporters, due to lifelong intimacy with cigarettes and alcohol, had little singing ability and less enthusiasm. One of them asked if the distinguished businessman was attempting to distract them from their investigative duties. To this Pettypoint said no, forty times, in as many different voices.

A murmur rustled through the crowd, and one radio

newsman asked Pettypoint why he had summoned the press to so unorthodox a free meal. Gripping the lectern and swaying visibly, the great figure answered in words that have become a household joke in most Wall Street offices: "Because, Mister Dudley, God has loaned the world to his teenage son, and we'd better get ready for the smashup."

Pettypoint lost consciousness and was rushed to the Thompson Clinic for Needless Expense in nearby Evanston. Here he was elaborately tested and so billed for such discomforts as bullet wounds, poison, paper cuts, cat bites, and rapture of the deep. Doctors x-rayed him extensively and even traced his body on tagboard with colored pencils. No possible expense was avoided to determine his condition. He had been reduced to the world's third richest man before the medical profession was satisfied that Pettypoint had suffered a nervous breakdown and not, in fact, frostbite. Meanwhile, the press had exploited the incident by playing up Pettypoint's sacrilege, and the *Daily News* proclaimed MILLIONAIRE CLAIMS TO KNOW GOD'S PLANS. The National Council of Churches met to discuss returning the five million dollars Pettypoint had given them a month earlier, and finally resolved instead to maintain an icy silence on the subject. Hate mail from small towns filled the insurance magnate's hospital room, and one student nurse (a Catholic) attempted to encase his head in Scotch tape while he slept. She was routed, however, by her intervening bedtime.

After a week of sedation and foods that began with the letter *c*, Pettypoint was dismissed to the care of his personal servants, who drove him home in one of the leftover automobile costumes. Once in his own bed, he resumed control of his business, which had been supervised in his seven-day absence by a succession of vice-presidents, each of whom had shot his predecessor and enjoyed a few heady hours in office. (The phone bills these interim leaders had piled up later proved to be the single greatest operating expense in Pettypoint's fiscal career.) Kitty returned from Acapulco, where she had gone to pray for her husband's recovery, tanned and ready to serve him. To assist her in this service she brought back with her three lithe Mexican youths in the first brown blush of manhood.

Pettypoint was by no means completely recovered. He never explained or apologized for his quixotic behavior and expressed only a desire to see the photographs of the ice sculptures that the caterers had provided. Though bedridden, he continued to oversee all his corporation's interests, and for reference used toy Civil War soldiers spread on his blankets to represent the various departments and factions under his control. Kitty, careful to avoid the contagion some associate with nervous breakdowns, kept herself and the three Mexican youths protectively confined in the guest house behind the mansion.

In March of 1954, Pettypoint returned to his offices but lasted only three weeks. Complaining about the ventilation one day, he supposedly remarked to his aide Byron Wheeler, "Any damn thing could come buzzing out of those air vents—tsetse flies, gnats, cicadas. It's distracting." The office atmosphere became strained by his insistence on affecting a beekeeper's outfit at all times.

There was no real need for him to go back to work. He had more money than he and an expressly hired staff of imaginative people knew what to do with. He issued memoranda telling his staff to refer to coffee as "tea," and to call sugar "beets," in order (said the memo) to maintain office security. For several days in April he fired articles of office furniture and instructed Byron Wheeler to show them to the door. Finally, the second breakdown, long feared by those who did not stand to profit by it, necessitated Pettypoint's discreet abdication from regular involvement in the affairs of the company he owned.

Testifying for a Senate committee that April, he denounced Communists with what newsmen called "a provocative dance" and fled to the lap of the Lincoln Memorial, where he named a lost boy scout his heir. Twelve-year-old Jimmy Hubbard was disqualified a day later, when it was learned his parents were foreigners with glasses.

The medical and journalistic worlds returned their attention to Pettypoint, and once again he proved a lucrative enigma for both. He was flown back to New York and entered a private clinic there with his wife, who was under treatment for lockjaw. Tests of his brain definitely located it in his head, but beyond that the experts could only conjecture for a half fee. One surgeon suggested "a broken heart" as the cause of the millionaire's troubles, but, though widely praised by critics, the theory was ultimately rejected. Pettypoint himself seemed to link his idiosyncrasies with his hard-won wealth. "I seem crazy because I'm the only man on earth who doesn't need to impress anybody. I'm not overtired, I'm overrelaxed," he wrote in a letter to fourteen-year-old Mimi Gillis, notifying her that she had been chosen at random from her high school register to be his successor.

While resting at the clinic, he began working on his memoirs, though his love for secrecy was such that even sixteen years later all that his publishers had to show the public was five hundred pages of erasures. Mimi Gillis was flown to the New York offices and tutored in English (her family had changed its name) while Pettypoint arranged for an official passing-the-crown ceremony in the New York Stock Exchange. Though confined to his room, he spent hours writing telegrams every day, and communicated with his aides by flipping the venetian blinds in code. When a complicated office intrigue required Mimi to go away to have a baby, he was depressed by the delay and promptly chose another potentially promising unknown from the records of the Des Moines public schools, this time a hyperactive child with a history of arson. Timmy Frayne was the youngest Fate had ever ordained for his successor (ten), but Pettypoint, aware that he could never return to the helm, rushed his protégé through a combined course on table manners and great Civil War strategies. Timmy received the mantle of leadership for all the Pettypoint enterprises at the gala Wall Street ceremony originally intended for Jimmy or Mimi, on July 19, 1954. The business has flourished unprecedentedly in the three decades since his accession.

Pettypoint was now free to become as squirrelly as he pleased. His divorce from Kitty shocked the social world (or at least it looked shocked in order to get free drinks), but he generously granted her possession of all the objects in the house that looked like her. Her later troubles are well known but really not that interesting. Her own autobiography, *Pile Your Plate, There's No Second Helpings,* offers this insight into their separation:

> The lawyer came to visit us with his little black
> bag, and because we hated each other so much,
> God gave us a beautiful tiny divorce out of that
> hate. And that's where divorce comes from.

Bachelor trappings quickly became the style at the mansion. The refrigerator was filled with beer and butter pecan ice cream, and even the servants felt free to leave their dirty socks and underwear on stairways or by the telephone. Junk autos, skeletons of moose and deer, and souvenir World War I helmets and memorabilia adorned the larger rooms. In all these Pettypoint took little interest; in fact, the new look was created by Guido del Ringo, a decorator hired to erase Mrs. Pettypoint's memory from the house. In the process del Ringo also inadvertently erased several Titians and the view from one picture window, but Pettypoint counted any overkill as worth the price.

Slowly the famous Pettypoint preoccupation with his own bodily functions began to manifest itself. The hygienic urge that had prompted him to don beekeeping togs now flourished in his solitude and self-absorption. He hired a squad of artists to render their conceptions of various vistas of the inside of his body. Most of these remain in litigation with the rest of the estate, but one, *The Lungs at Twilight*, can be seen in the lobby of the Pettypoint Plaza in Chicago.

His concern about bacterial infection grew so morbid that he refused to eat anything that had been inside his mouth. More and more of his staff were sent away, and those who, in a manner of speaking, remained were required to do all the housekeeping via the mails, never in person.

His paranoia proliferated. In November of 1966 he became convinced that his two German shepherd guard dogs, Dutch and Frieda, were secretly attempting to evolve to a more intelligent species and thereby take over the Pettypoint operations. The dogs were arrested and held on suspicion for "a period not to exceed eighty million years" in order for the local police department to see if there was any evidence supporting the millionaire's "willful evolution" charge. The dogs died in captivity without issue, and the charges were dropped.

From 1975 onward, rumors of Pettypoint's death abounded, and *Billboard* magazine named him as the "Most Possibly Dead But No One's Sure" personality for three consecutive years. The *National Enquirer* ran a series of articles supposedly written by his personal valet, but a major press scandal revealed that they had in fact been free-lance material concocted by Jacqueline Onassis pending her first book contract. Public curiosity about his activities reached a peak when he had the city of New York evacuated for a one-week period in August of 1976. When residents returned, many found their personal photo albums rearranged and leftover fried chicken in the refrigerator. Byron Wheeler affirmed to *Times* reporters that Pettypoint was indeed alive, but added that effigies in beekeeper outfits were often mistaken for him for weeks at a time.

In March of 1977 the federal agents assigned to sifting through Pettypoint's garbage contracted trichinosis, prompting the government to suspend surveillance activities until a hardier strain of G-man could be developed. At the time of the suspension, records show that whoever was living inside the Pettypoint house was eating exclusively Chinese take-out food and Easter candy. Airplane parts and secondhand cyclotrons were also noted in the estate's trash cans, causing some speculation that Pettypoint was considering personal military expansion. Following the confusion wrought by the trichinosis tragedy, Pettypoint's activities were shrouded in mystery until official word of his death came on June 5, 1977.

Pettypoint was found in the tub, where he had been abandoned because the staff assumed he was an effigy in a beekeeper's coat. The autopsy was conducted on Harris Bottleman, Pettypoint's public relations director, since the tycoon had specified in his will that his body was to be examined only by proxy. The coroner ruled that according to his evidence, Pettypoint had been dead for ten to fifteen years, but admitted that "it might be the aftershave he was wearing" that gave that effect.

The enigmatic figure's remains were scattered to the winds a week later, frustrating some who said they would dance on his grave, although one intrepid adversary attempted to skydive through his smoke as it rose from the crematorium. The will was simple. Kitty received autographed pictures of herself; Byron Wheeler was given "any perishables whatsoever that remain in the house, including flowers." One million dollars were allocated to the Society for the Promotion of Perpendicular Interment (he had always wished to conserve space) and another million to the People's Crusade to Remove the Letter J from the Alphabet. The remainder of his one-and-a-half-billion-dollar estate was distributed evenly among four schoolchildren in Santa Fe, New Mexico, who had been chosen at random about a year earlier. It was later learned that Pettypoint rewrote his will every six months, always inserting the names of different arbitrarily determined youngsters, and always changing the selection when any of them reached the age of fifteen.

"Maybe it was his way of saying thanks to all the children who bought Orphans' Insurance in the thirties," offers biographer Jared Weinstein, whose only work is a life of Harriet Beecher Stowe and whose suppositions are negligible. "Children seemed to play an important role in his life, though I don't know. Little Eva, now there was a child."

"His life was his statement," said newsman Wiley Cragg the day after Pettypoint's death. "I think he was asking whoever it was to repeat the question."

if u cn rd ths, u r prbly a secy and shdnt b rdng ths bk

All men feel an habitual grati-
tude, and something of an hon-
ourable bigotry, for the objects
which have long continued to
please them.
—William Wordsworth

As children, when the closest thing to a power possession was a Jetsons' lunchbox, few of us really imagined that eventually we'd sit in a nine-by-twelve room all day every day, suck up quarts of coffee, or (unless we attended the right boarding schools) fill out expense-account vouchers. Neither did we dream of having, after Mom, a person under our control whose job it was to smile pleasantly and arrange our lives. Secretaries, for better or (more probably) worse, were a nonexistent childhood category. But with adulthood finally came offices, caffeine, knowing who Pliny the Elder was, a lot of keys, and the realization that secretaries are the greatest invention since and including Brie wheels.

Lacking a personal secretary, you might as well forget those dreams of respectability and slide back into your old career working the sheepgut-drying bins at the racket factory. A secretary to call one's own is the sine qua non of success and power in America.

But you don't resemble Cary Grant and chances are the person who fetches your memos won't look like Miriam Hopkins or even Gale Storm. After all, this is 1980. And a secretary today needn't even be a woman. No, anybody—man *or* woman—who is reliable, precise, hard-working, and cooperative, has the makings of a good secretary, just so long as she doesn't spend *all* her time doing her nails and then go and get pregnant six months after being hired.

Male secretaries—or, in technical business language, "uncreative homosexuals"—no longer provoke quizzical reaction. Employers are now aware that secretaries who happen to be named Ralph or Harvey can crank out paperwork with the best of them.

Some think it inevitable that male and female secretaries will be treated differently. To measure this supposed differential (and a lot of other things), we commissioned an experiment, conducted two years ago by a registered* sociologist under the rigid sanctions laid down by the American Association of Legitimate Experimenters. Covert tape recordings were made of all boss-secretary interactions that occurred during one week at the headquarters of a large manufacturer of cat poisons. Reprinted below are two transcripts from the many hours thus recorded. We've deleted, however, all references to the secretaries' respective genders. With the telltale words expunged, not *one* of our re-

---

*Under the laws of many states, "sociologist" is not an official registration category. In Idaho, where our experiment took place, "Democrat" was the closest available rubric.

search team could distinguish the dialogue involving the male secretary from the one with the girl. And we'll wager that you'll be unable to detect any difference either, if you know what's good for you.

TRANSCRIPT #29

Mr. Moorehead, Vice-President for Internal Re-Hash: Smith? Will you step into my office when you have a chance? I have some data on those new thermostatic control units I'd like you to take a look at.

M— Smith, Secretary: Right away, sir, as soon as I've finished ordering the audio visual equipment you wanted.

(a pause in the recording)

Moorehead: Yeah, sit down, Smith. Say, did you see—no, you can sit there, just move the condoms—did you see the 76ers game last night on the tube? Jesus friggin' Christ, that Dr. J sure can shoot, can't he?

Smith: No shit, sir. *Three* guards had a tough time coverin' him.

Moorehead: Now, Smith, about this column of test figures here—

Smith: The copper stress coefficients, Mr. Moorehead?

Moorehead: Right, right, whatever you call them. Now, do you think I've got to put *all* those *numbers* on the big color charts for the sales meeting on Thursday? I mean, they kinda confuse me . . .

Smith: If I were you, sir, I'd just include them in the mimeographed handout material.

Moorehead: Okay, fine, sounds super to me. Great. Hey, uh, Smith, on your way out would you send in one of the _____ to make me a sandwich?

TRANSCRIPT #94

Mr. Andrews, Executive Comptroller for Toxin Development: Uh, M—Rizzi, would you slip into something more comfortable?

M— Rizzi, Secretary: Sir?

Andrews: My *office*. My office is a lot more comfortable than your cubicle, get it? (A male snigger is heard on the tape.)

Rizzi: I'll be right in, sir. But first I'd better finish ordering the mink coat for your mistress and licking clean the Mr. Coffee machine.

(long pause in the recording)

Andrews: Have you sent out all the letters I gave you this morning?

Rizzi: No, um, Mr. Andrews, I mean—the correspondence is all finished, but it hasn't been Xeroxed yet. The machine's jamming.

Andrews: Not much of a knack for electronics, eh? I'll get one of the _____ up from maintenance to fix it.

Rizzi: No, it's just that the feeder control bar is *worn out,* it's—

Andrews: Feeder control bar, M— Rizzi? What are you talking about? You just stick to repairing the runs in your _____, okay?

The moral of all this? Some executives know precisely how to handle a secretary, while others badly fumble the job of "office parent." Just as no one is a born stenographer, proper secretary-rearing doesn't come instinctively to many of us otherwise destined for corporate power.

Every would-be office worker still requires—*and wants*—the kind of firm-but-loving instruction that you'd routinely lavish on a little cocker puppy fresh from the pet store. And since most secretaries arrive reasonably house-trained and come running to sustained high-pitched whistles, you're two steps ahead of the secretarial obedience game. (Indeed, in the happy but unlikely event that your office tasks consist exclusively of fetching sticks and resisting baths, you need not read further. Just load up the canteen vending machines with Gainesburger salad plates and watch productivity skyrocket.)

But let's suppose you've never had your own secretary before. Oh, sure, you've long had a pro rata right to the sloppy seconds of the steno pool, but you've forever craved monogamy, a chipper doer of menial tasks who's true to you alone. And now, thanks to your well-earned promotion (after all, you never once failed to call your boss "Serene Highness," even in the third person), the invisible hierar-chical hand has meted out that most crucial appurtenance. The joyous day has arrived, and none too soon. "Go ahead, Joe," your superiors say, "and get yourself a *secretary.*"

Once your pliable piece of human capital is in hand, what in the heck are you supposed to *do* with him or her for eight long hours, five days a week? Many neophytes in their distress have tried dictating fictitious letters to nonexistent customers, ordering new secretaries to retype long passages of the Old Testament or the 1971 Endangered Species Act, or having them requisition unneeded truckloads of mi-crofiche emulsifier. Within a week or two you'll no doubt tire of contriving pointless task after pointless task just to save face and make your *desire* for a secretary appear a *need.* Take a pointer from the cruel king: he had only to think up *one* chore to keep Sisyphus busy for years. It might not do to have your administrative assistant spend each weekday pushing a large stone up to the thirty-eighth floor, but comparable and more seemly alternatives abound. For instance, that your secretary can't see the *sense* in transcribing and enlarging on poster-board every word you utter is no reason not to give the galling order. You've realized now that you don't strictly "need" a full-time secretary like cells need oxygen, but if you don't exercise your prerogatives, who will? Management is your job, and management means giving orders, the more the better. Hesitation for any reason can send your precarious house of cards fluttering to the dirt.

We can't tell you how many times one of these panicky Success Clinic graduates has called our relatively toll-free number and screamed, "Hey, guys, *what's what?*" We've dealt with the most common problems below.

How Much Should I Pay My Secretary?

College was supposed to have taught you how to ask the right questions. And as regards secretarial remuneration, the right question is not "how *much*" but "whether or not." Loads of eager young people are willing to work long hours for little or no pay, just for the chance to get a foot in the door of exciting "glamour" industries like heavy equipment resale or gypsum pulverization. However, with the unfortunate decline of the ethic of work for work's sake, most employees now insist on at least an occasional paycheck. But secretaries, like children and streetwalkers, quickly lose respect for an overseer who overpays. A convenient equation we recommend fixes a secretary's annual salary at no more than 90 percent of your previous year's expenditure on liquor and mouthwash.

How Old Should My Secretary Be?

There is no one "right" age for a secretary. While "administrative assistants" are without exception assertively youthful and "executive secretaries" tend to have reached menopause concurrent with President Kennedy's assassination, a simple secretary may be of any age. Piaget demonstrates in his famous clinical study that as early as six months of age a secretary is fully able to distinguish between a water cooler and a parent; at five years understands that a half-full glass of Diet Pepsi is actually half empty; and by the time he or she reaches puberty comprehends why men do all the important work in the office.

Do Secretaries Require Special Schooling?
No, they require special genes.

But Can't Education Help at All?
The basic secretarial skills can, of course, be taught. But more important, *attitudes* can be learned. Just as *you* can't begin too early scooping out the obstacle course standing in the way of *real* success, a secretary's predisposition for her sort of "success" may be nurtured by formal means. In most of our larger cities, where sidewalks are equally dense with secretaries and common pigeons on their respective lunch hours, the Yellow Pages are overstuffed with listings for "Secretaries" and "Secretaries, Schools for." (Beware: The telephone company's imprecision about the former has led several executives-in-a-rush to hire fragile seventeenth-century antique desks to answer their phones and open mail, usually with disappointing results.) The phone book broadsides for the myriad schools range from six-year degree-granting institutions with seminars on "The Semiotics of Speedwriting," to dog-eared back-room walk-ups full of broken Underwoods, dusty paper, and a faculty of renegade Avon ladies. In filling our own staff vacancies, we've had the best luck with the Montessori secretarial schools. The Montessori system encourages the development

of the secretary's own initiative, and the better graduates can type letters before you've dictated them, make appointments with clients you don't yet have, and buy anniversary presents for your spouse even if you're single. In addition, Montessori-trained secretaries are able to dress themselves, understand simple fractions, and speak a language something like Italian.

What if My Secretaries Misbehave?
Although many companies now discourage corporal punishment officially, a quiet spanking in the stockroom can generally quash the first indications of secretarial delinquency. On the other hand, if you—like most successful people—are disgusted by the thought of physical contact of any kind, subtler discipline may be in order. Try waiting until that errant receptionist/file clerk has a serious accident before you reveal that those "medical benefits" promised by personnel consist in fact of free aspirin and the unlimited use of a toy stethoscope. And we understand, too, that electric typewriters can be wired in such a way as to emit harmless electric shocks.

How Should I Reward Good Behavior?
If a secretary has been especially competent, a big gooey brownie might be appropriate recompense, and in extraordinary circumstances—say, when your secretary has labored nonstop for 120 hours doing work for which you'll take all the credit—you might consider springing for a season pass to the Ice Capades.

ENOUGH
TO KNOW
BETTER

---

*Youth does not require reasons
for living, it only needs pretexts.*
—José Ortega y Gasset

"In a way, I guess you could say I'm changing things from
the *inside* now," explained successful feedback administrator Rod Sampson one afternoon last fall. "You know,
synergy." Sampson, a boyish (but no longer puckish) thirty-
two, stroked the tips of his floppy mustache and glanced out
over the glittering wedge of Chicago's Loop that lay below
his forty-eighth-floor office. Rod is obviously proud of the
material appurtenances of success—the five-figure tax pay-
ments, the Jacuzzi dishwasher, the architect-designed backyard gazebo where his children stay during Rod's bimonthly
custody periods. But young Rod Sampson, a mover-and-
nearly-a-shaker, is acutely sensible too of the intangible re-
wards of his "life after the sixties thing, the whole new
frame of mind *everyone* has." Serving refreshments from
his Mr. Cappuccino machine, Rod recounts an anecdote to

---

make his point about "the heavy changes" the corporate universe has undergone.

"Like just the other day, I turned on my assistant for the first time." A virgin betrayal? "No, man, *turned him on,* got him high. The dude is fifty, had never *seen* a joint before, he's into the whole suburban trip, everything. We were down there by the keypunch stations, and he takes a toke, likes it, takes a few more—the guy was getting high. And then he asks me—get this—he asks me with a straight face, 'Rod, what kind of calculator should I buy for my tax work?' Now get behind *that*: what kind of *calculator* for his *taxes*."

Rod Sampson smiled and shook his head in remembered disbelief. He snuffed out his Kent Golden Light 100, careful to extinguish the last ember (*"Hate* it when they lie there and *smolder,* you know?"). "Now I was just blown away. This old dude *did not know* that the Hewlett-Packard four-two-niner is the only microprocessor package to go with. The primo unit. Doesn't have an accountant do his ten-forty, either. Wow." Rod paused. "I was tempted to goof on him, but you know," he reflected finally and gently, with the frank insight typical of his generation, "that's what I really like about reefer. It makes people *honest*."

Rod Sampson is not unlike the hundreds of thousands of young people who've turned in their beards for brains, love beads for briefcases, and bell-bottoms for more expensive bell-bottoms. According to the 1970 census, 3,289,000 Americans between the ages of sixteen and twenty-nine described themselves as "very hip" or "somewhat hip," and a comparable number claimed to "know what's hip," or "use the word life-style" at least twice a week. During the ensuing decade—as selling out came to mean merger or acquisition—a goodly proportion of those three-million-plus hipsters became second lieutenants (if not captains) of industry. It may seem an impossible leap of faithlessness from the communal crash-pad to the private sector, but remember that Woodstock was a business venture and that "prophet" and "profit" are pronounced the same.

As one leading employer of Vietnam protest veterans told us, "Ounces of pot, or machine tool parts, what's the difference? Selling is selling. When you think about it, the moratorium marches were just conventions with armbands instead of 'HELLO, I'M KEITH' badges, and without funny hats or hookers."

We can only speculate at how many Rod Sampsons now walk the bright corridors of corporate America. There are clues aplenty, from master's programs in "Multinational Mellowness" and "Life-Enhancing Accountancy," to the phenomenally increasing sales reported by the Association of Tinted Eyeglass and Cokespoon Necklace Manufacturers for the last several fiscal years. The plains are dotted with geodesic slaughterhouses, and Jaycee-sponsored Rolfing sessions for middle management are common. To paraphrase Bob Dylan, today's former youth are not following leaders, they're buying parking meters. Indeed, they now *own* Maggie's farm, and Alice's Restaurant is a franchise operation.

A WALL STREET
FIGHTING MAN

Take Josh Menzies. On any given afternoon in 1968, Josh might be found on an Ann Arbor street corner, a stick of mediocre grass in one hand, dozens of ill-considered leaflets clutched in the other. Josh thought himself constantly "living on the edge," although when pressed he could only cite his failure to study for the law boards and the time he stole a Sly Stone album as evidence for his existential outlawry.

Josh experienced his first disillusionment with counter-cultural hegemony upon graduating from college. "I realized I needed a job. But it was like a Catch-22, you know? You had to have experience to get a job, but you couldn't get experience unless you had a job." Finally Josh landed an entry-level position with the Menzies Metals and Chemicals Corporation. Though it was a dulling routine job managing a nitrate refinery, Josh worked hard to play by the straight world's rules, even cutting his waist-length blond hair and agreeing to arrive at work no later than noon. "I was really paranoid at first," he says. "You know, it was like a Catch-22: I had to look like Mr. White-Collar Conservative to get along, but I couldn't get along without looking like Mr. White-Collar Conservative." His only previous experience with chemical sales was desultory and entailed little more than accurate measurement of gram weights. His fortunes at the company plummeted, however, when it was discovered that Josh had begun diluting outgoing shipments of fertilizer with substantial quantities of powdered milk and baking soda in order to increase the profits.

Josh finally came to feel unprepared for the rigors of corporate management, and decided to return to school for a graduate business degree. Though he completed his coursework, Josh withdrew from school just before commencement and never received his M.B.A. "You know, I never cared about a piece of *paper* that says you're educated, anyway. It was sort of a Catch-22 situation, right? You had to write a dissertation to get the degree, but then you also had to work really hard to get good grades." His half-completed thesis—"*Siddhartha* as a Model for Effective Human Relations Scenarios"—is bound in rawhide and sits on a stereo speaker in Josh's office.

These days you're likely to find Josh eating lunch ("no

red meat, *ever*'') in a posh Wall Street restaurant not far
from work. And work these days, for Josh, is being assistant director of the public affairs office of a major bank. ''I
deal with the media, whenever the media wants to know
something about our operations. Since most of the media
people are like me,'' Josh says, ''we get along real
smoothly. It's just like Vonnegut said—I think it was Vonnegut, maybe it was Castaneda—about doing the best you
can and not worrying too much. 'So it goes,' right?''

THE WHOLE WORLD
IS WATCHING

Marc Rosen's picture appeared in *Life* magazine eleven
years ago this fall. In that famous photograph, Marc sits in
an overstuffed chair in his college dean's office, reading the
administrator's private diary and idly shattering the man's
supply of insulin ampules. The caption reads: ''City College
junior Mark Rosen, one of the S.D.S. occupiers, in a play-
ful moment during the anti-test sit-in last week.''

A poster-sized reproduction of that photograph hangs
on the wall of Marc Rosen's Madison Avenue office today,
opposite a similarly enlarged version of Marc's decade-old
police mug shot. Rosen doesn't mention these relics to visitors, doesn't boast about them, but the copywriter's smirk-
ing glances from side to side leave no question about his
nostalgic pride.

''Now you're gonna ask if I think I've sold out, aren't
you?'' Rosen sputtered in the clipped, urgent tone not so
changed from the days when he was demanding nonnegotia-
bly that his faculty council rename the college snack bar
The Michael Bakunin Center for Students in Society. (In
fact, the facility has gone through two more name changes

since, from the Robert F. Kennedy Coordinating Area to today's Snack 'n' Study Place.) "Well, I'll tell you," Rosen continues, "we stopped a war and brought down two presidents. I was on the streets. I was arrested. I paid my dues. I was in Chicago [in April, 1973, at the annual meeting of the short-lived Caucus for a New Advertising] and Berkeley [to visit his law student girl friend two summers ago]. Just last spring I went to a Karen Silkwood fund-raiser at Ramsey Clark's niece's house, and I've met Bill Kunstler, personally. I'm still involved. I don't call that selling out. I call that being in a different space."

Rosen quickly warmed to us when we explained that we weren't about to pull out the tired charge of idealism betrayed, of "selling out." We wanted to know how his experience peddling half-baked radical notions had prepared him for the serious task of peddling half-baked consumerist messages.

"Yeah, *yeah*—that's what I always tell my social worker friend Barry. I'm doing the same thing I always was—communicating to the workingpeople and helping them improve their living standard—but in a new context. Contexts are very important to consider, you know."

Marc has very profitably recycled (his word) sixties catchphrases into usable eighties tools (also his word). There's Krieger beer's well-known advertising slogan:

At the end of the day, give peace a chance . . .
With a couple of Kriegers!

which Marc claims to have "conceptualized," and his imprint is unmistakable on the TransWest Aerospace Corporation's latest campaign:

The country's problems seem insoluble?
At TransWest, we shall overcome.

Marc was quick to point out a current project that makes him feel "real good, you know, *caring*." The project is a series of magazine ads sponsored by a leading American telephone company. The slogan:

In this great land, we need *integration.*
Racial and *vertical.*
Monopolies—they're just a different kind of togetherness.

We were moved by these bold sentiments and told Marc Rosen so as he gave us an oddly complicated handshake of farewell. Marc simply said, "Later," and returned to his plush-carpeted garret for another afternoon of effective communication and a quick memo to his muses.

24 FRAMES OF
MIND PER SECOND

Jocelyn Braithwaite's *Videotaped Mandala Series* and her autobiographical black-and-white film, *Westchester: An Oh-So-Pretty Nightmare,* caught the eye of a Public Broadcasting production executive while Jocelyn was still a senior at Bard College. The result was Braithwaite's only full-length work, *Yes, Virginia,* which purported to show the uncanny parallels between the seemingly disparate lives of Jocelyn Braithwaite and Virginia Woolf.

Eight years after *Yes, Virginia* was first broadcast, Jocelyn is still "creating, experiencing, growing." Growing especially fast and large are the sales of Braithwaite-designed home lighting systems, sold under the trade name Glōwz. Essentially a hookup of motion picture lighting equipment painted in bright primary colors (and marked up in price sixfold), Glōwz has made Jocelyn a wealthy young woman.

"Filmmaking was a beautiful way of relating to a certain historical moment," Braithwaite says now. "Those were grainy, black-and-white, high-contrast times. Now I like making beautiful things for people I like. That's how Glōwz came about." Making "beautiful things," along with her savvy decision to incorporate her holding company in the Bahamas for tax purposes, allows Braithwaite to pursue various creative endeavors without commercial stricture.

Jocelyn, who lives in seaside Venice, California, visits her corporate offices in downtown Los Angeles for a few hours a day, "just as a chance to clear out my head a little bit," and today to put finishing touches on the long-term sales strategy for her new venture. The enterprise, in its basics, foresees the sale of Indian-made pottery by means of a Tupperware-like merchandising network.

"Do you know *anyone* who'd go to a Tupperware party? I mean, *honestly*. Who wants plastic containers? (My Korean couple doesn't understand how they work, anyway.) But I thought that whole sort of decentralized infrastructure, a sort of sisterhood sales thing, I thought that could be viable for delivering beautiful objects that people really want, really need." If the initial sales of Native American crafts go well, Braithwaite says, the division (The Goods Collective, Inc.) will begin test-marketing reproductions of Balinese religious artifacts, bath soap made in a Kyoto "temple," and a line of Swedish-made designer contraceptives.

Is she still true to her first professional passion, the cinema? "As a matter of fact," she points out, her face a mask of seriousness and hyper-empathy, "I've just finished a thirty-minute documentary on the absolutely *horrible* conditions on the Navaho reservations in the Southwest. Now I'll grant you," she says, "some of their little huts are very *special* spaces. But the filth, the pestilence, the lack of decent opportunities for self-expression." Braithwaite shakes her long mane of tight curls. "I hope I conveyed some of that."

And when might we (or the people who go to these kinds of movies, anyway) expect to see the results of her searing exposé of others' problems?

"Well, we've signed like a dozen independent stations already in the major markets." A cunning half-hour *advertisement* in the form of a documentary? "Sort of. I mean we did focus a lot on the meticulousness of the pottery craftspeople, and how by selling their work wholesale to us they don't have to deal with the whole marketing hassle themselves. If that promotes people's consciousness of our Real Goods selling plan, far out. But selling is definitely not the bottom line here," Braithwaite asserts with eye contact that left us in envious awe. "The bottom line is the Native American experience."

Whither the sixties? Well, a few of the retailers among us had our gravy train derailed, stuck with warehouses full of passé Nehru jackets and "Haight-Ashbury" lunchboxes. (Although with new markets opening up in the modishness-starved Iron Curtain countries, some of us are looking to unload our leftover countercultural merchandise, and some of us have even made very lucrative overtures to certain trade envoys who claimed they could pull strings in Budapest, but have yet to make good on their bought-and-paid-for promises.) Others of us in the business of meeting shifts in public demand have had good luck; denim automobile upholstery, name-brand granola cereals, and "herbal" shampoos are register-ringing testimony to the fortune of some.

But if you're like us and are interested in the significance of the new generation in only the narrowest, utilitarian sense, you want two answers. First, you Depression children are eager to learn if you've reason to fear the cascade of youths into the job market. Yes and no. Some of these enviable cultural chameleons do possess the remarkable ability to take on the colors of the eighties—a shade of cool aquamarine ambition, made especially bright by an acid tint of nihilist self-apology—that should have them usurping your authority years before you're ready to retire. From the others—the Napa Valley midwives and bearded New Hampshire cabinetmakers, the young people who, in short, took the sixties seriously—you should feel little threatened. Indeed, before the century's out, our national servant problem ought to be nearly solved.

And what about you youth? Our research indicates that your earlier transgressions will *not* be held against you as you boogie on down the road to white-collar respectability. Wishing for satori and social change wasn't a sin; rather, consider the failure of the Woodstock Nation a negative test-market report. You've cut your losses. You've suffered through your midlife crises early.

Straighten that (narrow) tie and walk tall and proud toward the bright beacon light of Success, for all along, *we* knew what you thirsted for: All you were saying was "Give *me* a chance."

"HONEY, I'M

—AS PREVIOUSLY AGREED UPON"

No profit grows where is no pleasure ta'en.
—William Shakespeare

If you don't make time to enjoy, or to pretend to enjoy, a few civilized pleasures, others will think you a monumental brute. The highest echelons of power are open only to those apparently wholehearted few whose lives seem to shimmer serenely at every turn. A hayrack ride with the kids on a sunny afternoon in September, a snifter of fine brandy sipped slowly over an evening's rereading of *Buddenbrooks,* a wife who knows how you feel when you look at art— these are, of course, the conventional carrots-on-a-battery-of-sticks that were supposed to make worthwhile the forty-year-ache of career obsession. But that array of luscious dividends—tangible and less so—are means as well as ends.

Much as they'd prefer to, business chieftains can't go home to a pared-down chrome bachelor unit and spend every night honing their fiercest negotiating posture. No, there are stunning houses and responsibly pretty wives and overfed young ones. There are concerts and golf games and, within reason, good books. We've made it ungodly clear that an unstinting attention to *appearances* is the only thing close to a guarantee of success. And the obligation to appear heartily normal doesn't end at five-thirty every afternoon. If you must spend the whole of each workday being an anxious drudge—*and you must*—then the remainder of each twenty-four-hour period must be spent countering that impression of assiduous woodenness.

YOUR HOUSE

This is where most strivers commit their first glaring error. The innate urge to "keep up with the Joneses" is fine as far as it goes. But to distinguish yourself and your family from the countless thousands who exercise their brand-name fetish identically, whose credit cards and received sense of style are interchangeable with yours, you'll need more. You'll need what we call *acquisitive vision*. What this comes down to is keeping up with a sort of *Platonic ideal* of the Joneses. It's not enough to buy an expensive, unremarkable house in a fashionable suburb where black people choose not to live—even if that's precisely how all your associates have chosen their residences. For if you begin maintaining a material parity with a *specific* "Jones" family, or even a circle of them, you will soon be identified as one more faceless family of conforming Joneses. What you want is a transcendent amalgam of architectural styles. During your first week in a new city, order your wife or husband to take the small, concealable camera you've bought for the purpose and stroll unobtrusively around the acceptable neighborhoods—there are rarely more than two—taking snapshots of the homes of your prospective associates. Commission a discreet architect to design a house incorporating the most assertively soothing features of your dozen or so prototypes. This will be your new home regardless of your own aesthetic preferences.

Without quite knowing why, your new colleagues will experience a deep sense of reassuring familiarity in your house, and yet you will have sidestepped the dangerously lower-middle-class connotations of rote duplication. And if your artistic friends from college happen to visit, you'll have the satisfaction of describing yours as the "*only* postmodernist" structure in this "whole damn ticky-tacky neighborhood." When they ask why, in that case, you choose to live in a segregated, stultifyingly proper part of town, you need only mumble something about "great schools, progressive superintendent" and they'll be off your back instantly, ignoring the fact that your children attend private schools.

Since your older children have long since taken to laughing at you when asked to do chores and since neither you nor your spouse have the inclination to spend every weekend pruning, mowing, weeding, and fertilizing, a gardener is essential. Yet in many professional neighborhoods, it is considered highly appropriate that one's teenage sons make regular, lavish shows of physical labor. Thus, a gardener who looks *as if he could be* your offspring is recommended, despite the premium prices such adolescent doppelgängers fetch. And naturally, in this case, it would be unwise to employ the customary illegal alien unless very good tans and extreme bilingualism run in your family.

YOUR MATE

It's unavoidable that during spring your fancy turns to thoughts of love. But by the sweltering summer of your life, the glare of imperative success overhead, "love" and two bits will almost get you a *Wall Street Journal*. On the job you'd be thought a fool to buy new industrial equipment on the basis of some ephemeral hankering, or because you day-dreamed about the seductive tilt of its cams. The same, no-nonsense criteria you use at work obtain for your mating choice, even more so since capital depreciation allowances don't apply and you'll never have to kiss a forklift good night.

Although it wouldn't be unwise to bear in mind our suggested approach to housing here in the spouse depart-ment—the same as everybody else's, only better—the im-precision of human archetypes makes a strict application impossible. Rather, you should be aware of the **Basic Spouse Editions** into which an acceptable corporate husband or wife may fall. Only in the recording and motion picture in-dustries do these categories not pertain. The permitted di-vorce frequency in those fields makes it less important to choose mates with care and discrimination. Indeed, one middle-aged record executive we know is wont to refer to his third (late) wife as "number three with a bullet."

THE MAUREEN DEAN PORCELAIN ROBOT. As the wife of a small, weasellike man who published a book called *Blind Ambition,* Mrs. Dean is a perfect exemplar for this top-of-the-line conservative version. Such a spouse is obsessed with personal hygiene and attractive canapés, and will thus meet your needs accordingly. On the downside: she's liable to squander enormous amounts of time and money at Lilly Pulitzer, and baroque expressions of repressed emotional disturbance become a distinct possibility after age forty. While she is somewhat more than likely to engage in extramarital dalliances, you will have the consolation of knowing that your cuckolder derives no sensual pleasure from the liaison.

THE GOOD-NATURED FRUMP. This is certainly the most purely efficient choice. In the charge of this edition, your house will smell perpetually lemon-fresh, your meals will be plenteous and punctual (albeit undistinguished), and your offspring shielded from all manner of grit. Unfortunately, as your colleagues begin trading in their own first wives for cellulite-free young lookers, your Good-Natured Frump can become an embarrassing minor albatross. But except for the rare company functions at which she drinks too much and winks at your crotch, this well-meaning little tub seems unsatisfactory only in the cold light of day, when you consider what-might-have-been.

THE OVEREDUCATED HARRIDAN. It's easy to judge her harshly, but all this self-pitying snipe is doing is applying your own thoughtless arrogance to the family sphere. These women are either fat or covered in taut, mean flesh. They function best as traveling companions (instinctively knowing the best museums and restaurants to have visited) and as canny powers-behind-your-throne, since they have little to occupy their considerable intellect but schemes to better the circumstances of the mirror of their reflected glory (i.e., you).

There are just two castes of corporate husbands, though owing to the only semiexplored terrain of female moguldom, each contains more latitude than their distaff opposites.

THE BENUMBED CHUMP.   He is the boy you met senior year just after breaking up with that exquisitely heart-
breaking soccer star who wrote prize-winning poetry. You
were drained and resigned; your future husband was courte-
ous (i.e., never insisted on oral sex), kind (always provided
competent oral sex), and endowed with a responsibly diversified portfolio of table manners, securities, and real estate.
The *Times* ran your engagement announcement above the
fold with a twenty-four-point headline (CYNTHIA CROSBY,
BANKER, AFFIANCED TO BANKER), and he doesn't make a
peep when your seventy-hour work-weeks leave you ex-
hausted and rude for days at a time. In short, he fulfills the
same function as the Porcelain Robot, with the added bonus
of an income sufficient to redecorate the beach house every
other year. (One caveat: When he reaches his midthirties,
keep all alumni newsletters, handguns, and prescription
drugs quietly locked away.)

THE COLLEAGUE.   You may not be able to wear each
other's clothing, but your psychic sizes are identical in
every cut and tuck. His-and-her briefcases, a husband-and-
wife commuter car pool, exchanged tales of deal-cutting
around the dinner table—the two of you are flip sides of the
same shiny coin. There is the danger of cutthroat business-
world tactics seeping over into your highly charged married
life—with both of you vying for the Power Side of the bed,
say—but you'll have the convenience of never having to
dampen your power-seeking fires for the sake of coquettish
appearances. With a male version of your ambitious self for
a mate, you'll have the much-sought luxury of "a husband
who's also a best friend." You would, that is, if you didn't
find the very notion of a "best friend" laughable and naive.

YOUR CHILDREN

If the annual $750 tax break isn't adequate incentive for producing children, consider the unbounded opportunity for managerial experimentation. Before you go public with your novel notion for productivity rewards, say, try a dry run in the one realm where yours is the unassailable authority, and where mistakes and misfires won't damage your chances for advancement. Labor-management logjams aren't a problem at home, and if one of your progeny should develop into a four-foot-tall charismatic rabble-rouser, a smart spanking will remind everybody who's boss.

If proper inculcation doesn't begin early, a decade hence you will be faced with sons and daughters who spitefully reject you and your fundamental values (whatever *they* are). In the ideal corporate household, purposeless amusements like crossword puzzles, solitaire, and coloring books are prohibited. Don't be timid about asking your child *why* he is doing something, to what *end* he's "cutting out pretty magazine pictures." A boy or girl can't have too many erector sets, on the other hand, and make sure there are plenty of tall, clean stacks of play money around during the formative years.

The issue of subcontracting your child-rearing obligations remains controversial. And while we cannot unconditionally recommend any single route short of complete abdication (pleasant and clean orphanages *do* exist), we know of one immensely successful halfway alternative. Camp Strive, located in the former headquarters of an asbestos manufacturer on the shores of Lake Erie, is no ordinary "summer camp." Indeed, the facility is open to full-time campers only during the resolve-strengthening winter months. (The camp directors determined early on that for the tempering of young managerial souls, warm sun and summer breezes were an inappropriate climatic metaphor.) Camp Strive, according to their colorful brochure, seeks "to provide a total junior-corporate experiencing environment for young managers from three to twelve." While some conventional camp activities are on the Camp Strive agenda—cost-benefit lifesaving techniques, mass production of lanyards and "arrowheads"—the emphasis is on skills and attitudes unique to the business world the campers (or "strivers") will later join. Each reinforced-concrete cabin represents a Fortune 500 company, and the strivers from each are obligated to "maximize the profits" of his or her "company." "Gross revenues" are accumulated through success at camp sports and games, and through the takeover of competing cabin-companies. (The campers of these acquired units are sent without provisions into the forest for three nights, all alone, where they must find new venture capital financing.) The camp season winds up in mid-February, when all the several hundred strivers compete in an every-child-for-himself all-day game of Capture the Logo. Lightweight suits and ties are required wear for Camp Strive attendees at all times, and whimpering is not permitted.

YOUR FRIENDS

Whether or not adult men and women "really" have friends in the sense of people they can trust not to sleep with their lovers or steal their jokes is not only beyond the scope of this book, but as fundamentally irrelevant to the questions we need to address as the question of whether an unobserved electron "really" has position and momentum, or whether beef cattle "really" mind being slaughtered. We

employ the term "friend" in accordance with widely accepted current usage denoting (1) a person of one's own sex
with whom one has shared a lewd remark or an illegal drug,
or (2) a mere acquaintance who has a real chance of becoming famous.

For men it is wise not to expect too much out of the
manipulation of friends. Bosses, and women, even the slow
ones, can usually keep tabs on which one of you is the attractive, talented friend and which one of you is you. They
will not confuse the two of you, even if you wear his aftershave. It is also important to remember that a boorish, attractive, and talented friend should not become a role model
for you. The behavior that an individual can get away with
is tailored with extraordinary precision to his own sexual,
social, and financial leverage. If you cultivate the cocky im-
petuousness of your favorite screen actor, your friends will
throw you in the path of a train.

A good way to test the personality/leverage ratio is to
observe old people. In them, the personality of youth per-
sists, coasting along on pure inertia, long after their mori-
bund leverages—beauty, wealth, wit, and influence—have
dropped by the wayside. Their relatives can judge them in
the abstract, with an eye unjaundiced by their genetic and
legal inheritances. This is why the federal government must
enact programs to keep old people alive.

"If that's so," we're sometimes asked, "I mean, that
everyone's behavior is already the worst they can get away
with, then how can a book like this help anyone at all?"
"That is a terribly cynical attitude to adopt," we respond.

For women, a friend may be a girl's best friend.
Surely the most valuable office prop is an unattractive best
friend who provides the foil against which your modest ad-
vantages become serviceable. She must be unattractive
enough so that she dresses in a kind of Sensible Frowsy

look, embarrassed to enter a race she knows she can't win. It should be a woman who will have to devote her life to hard work, even altruism. A woman who will learn to find meaning in quiet stoicism, political activism, or twelve domestic cats. Confide to men that she's a wonderful, very special woman, but that you can't understand why she doesn't take care of herself—some event in her past, you suspect.

Sisterhood has its place, but maintain your leverage. Should a man betray a germ of interest in your friend, commence flirtation. Present him with the palpable alternative of your own gaping desire. When he speaks, list toward his mouth to bathe in the soothing audio current of his wisdom. When you've secured a tentative pass, snub him. Your friend will be too proud to accept what you've rejected. She doesn't need your hand-me-downs.

YOUR CULTURAL INTERESTS

LITERATURE. Don't be scared off by that fancy word; we're not suggesting that you read Tobias Smollett novels or minor symbolist poems. Among other things, such a prescription would violate one of our axial rules for success: *Eggheads don't get ahead*. But certain kinds of writing are better for you than others, just as certain vegetables and shirts can make your passage to power smoother.

Poems are fine—*in moderation*. Verse composed according to strict metrical form is preferable, since it helps reinforce the importance of unvarying structure and order in the epic poem that is your own life. Herbert Sweeney Janstrom—the prolific poet laureate of Dearborn, Michigan—would be a good choice, and Janstrom's "O! Sweet Assembly Line of My Youth" a particularly untroubling example of his art. Aside from the classic works that contain specific instructional value (e.g., *The Merchant of Venice,* Act I), most books written before 1800 are more trouble than they're worth, as are any novels by an author whom no one's ever heard of. Otherwise, Dickens is good, for reminders of *why* you thirst for power (and in addition you'd be surprised at how often the word *Bildungsroman* crops up during high-level business conferences); if you can manage to read *Faust* with an open mind, Goethe is good, and German besides; Sinclair Lewis is enlightening in his quaint way—his work should particularly fascinate those of you searching for your roots. And any author whose books have sold more than a million copies in the last ten years—thus transforming him into a businessman, just like you—is probably a good bet. Musts to avoid: E. M. Forster, Marcel Proust, and Pablo Neruda, all of whom a reader of your station and temperament will find especially depressing.

MUSIC. Most of our clients have an inexplicable preference for Wagnerian imitators, or for the Italian semi-modernists—Puccini, Bellini, Mancini, and Mantovani. Our all-around suggestion is a good Sousa march, scored for guitar and vibraphone, played every evening just before dinnertime. Beware of evincing a fondness for movie soundtrack records; however, one sly investment banker we know regularly plays Strauss for new business associates, who invariably ask: "Is that the *original* '2001: A Space Odyssey' album?" Whereupon the host chuckles with just a hint of withering sneer.

ART. Careful now. It's a perilously thin line you'll have to tread between sissy and idiot, philistine and philanthropist. Impressionism is generally safe to enjoy, but better yet, just tag along on your wife's Junior League museum expeditions and you won't be led astray. Strongly recommended are gallery exhibitions such as the Tut treasures, attendant to which is such a degree of superfluous hoo-ha that even you will have something to talk about before, during, and after.

OPERA. Just *don't,* unless your company is an important local patron. Under such compulsory attendance you will, at least, be able to witness the most capital-intensive art form still extant, unless you consider computer manufacture an art.

YOUR SPORTS

For spectating, football is the obvious choice, particularly since the game's jargon is the lingua franca of today's powerbrokers. If your boss suggests making "a sneak end run around R. & D." or "handing off to the sales department right before the blitz," you'd be advised to reply in kind. A lacrosse-derived comeback, for instance, won't wash except in certain New England fiduciary syndicates, and metaphors with origins in roller derby or professional wrestling are inappropriate in most business situations. If you are a city dweller or Catholic, basketball is an acceptable second choice to football. And in certain circumstances—when you're entertaining the company's new equal opportunity compliance officer, for example—it's even better.

As for *participating* in sports, the only permissible endeavors are golf and any one of several racket sports. The choice in your case will depend on your professional field, your age, your area of the country, your systolic blood pressure, and whether or not you've got something to conceal in the way of obvious leg diseases. Squash is the finest popular sport for building competitive endurance, but those benefits are equaled by golf's promotion of boozy camaraderie between you and your social betters. (Jai alai is also terrific for developing ferocity, but unless you have your own backyard fronton, you'd better stick to the more conventional alternatives.)

An occasional hunting excursion is good for conveying an image of genial ruthlessness. In addition, by imagining your immediate superior's face on that fawn behind the cross hairs, your aggressive rage will be given more than merely symbolic vent. Yet in these manly pursuits, as well as in all organized sports and culture, remember that *leisure* has slightly different ground rules from *work*. In the fields and streams, *efficiency maximization* is no longer king, and you might be thought excessive if your companions see that you've brought along automatic weapons and gallons of defoliant. One of the authors knows from humiliating personal experience that it can be hard to explain away napalm-scorched pheasants as sorry victims of "some kinda rare fungus or something."

YOUR VACATIONS

At the very top, vacations are now rare. And for good reason. Vacations have always been hard, but today they are dangerous. Digs. Climbs. Expeditions. Somewhere along the line it was decided that one should spend one's leisure moments the way Jane van Lawick-Goodall does. While your life's work may center upon running market analyses on pinball bumper cushions, your vacation is expected to advance the frontiers of human knowledge or to test the limits of man's endurance. One popular vacation package is to sail an unseaworthy craft out into the ocean all alone, grow a beard, and radio a Coast Guard cutter to come and rescue you. Last year a graduate of our seminars established trade relations with a bush Negro tribe of Surinam while celebrating his fifteenth wedding anniversary.

Vacations are so strenuous and unpleasant that you may even spend them at home, so long as you reconstruct a viola da gamba and "catch up" on something you had let blissfully slide.

Most executives prefer not to hazard vacations anymore. Even sick leave is now viewed with mistrust.

YOUR PET

Just as the fully rounded businessman is expected to kill animals now and again, he must also demonstrate a sentimental interest in keeping one or two alive. Clearly, cats are out, even though their inscrutable stealth is an enviable model we might all like to emulate, and the dullest feline could teach us a thing or two about aloofness. But in their thoroughgoing covertness lies cats' unacceptability as corporate pets: who wants to keep an *animal* whose very being competes with you, and who nightly shames you with mute imperiousness?

A great big smelly dog is the obvious answer. Except for their vaguely Irish connotations, any of the retriever family make blue-chip family pets. Great Danes and Saint Bernards are fine if you are unperturbed by the idea of your small children being in constant danger of suffocation. An English sheep dog can be valuable for making yourself appear sleek and murderously keen by comparison. Collies, Airedales, German shepherds—any of the large, oafish species are appropriate, so long as they are trained to snarl at the underprivileged and to sit still once a year for the family Christmas-card portrait.

COPING
WITH
FAILURE

---

*I would prefer even to fail with
honor than win by cheating.*
                    —Sophocles

The book is nigh on winding up, and if everything has gone
according to our plan, you already feel the heady rush of
successability coursing through your once-limpid veins.

Yet there is another side. And if we failed to address
it, we would be as remiss in our comparatively sacred duty
as the seed salesman who didn't tell the first-time farmer
about the chance of hailstorms and locusts.

If we know nothing else, we know that every possibility implies its own opposite. We are born, yet we must die.
We may have the great good fortune to sire a flock of
bonny children, or we may be one of the many to discover
too late the folly of our modern ways, bombarded into
childlessness by the onslaught of *Happy Days* and micro-
wave forty-second baked potatoes. We naturally assume that a
coiled, lathering puma is *not* waiting for us behind that

closed bathroom door. But at the same time we must always be prepared for the *possibility* that some vicious jungle cat lurks in every darkened corner, waiting. If x exists, we may never properly rule out non-x (or even $-2x$).

And so it is with success. It doesn't take a genius to figure out success's alternative, the bleak bogeyman you try desperately to ward off with blustery displays of false gusto. Sure it gives you the shivers, and well it should.

We're talking *failure*.

Come on now, admit it: If your gut didn't tremble at the very thought of your own un-success, would you be angling right now for that power-infused corner office? Would you still spend furtive hours conniving to place just the right office objects and photographed loved-ones on your desk? Or practicing that intimidating snicker at the other fellow's mere mention of the word "Florsheim"? No. Just as you dream of success's sweet ambrosia, you can taste on your mind's tongue the rancid bitterness of defeat. Failure is real. Self-hate, the disapproval of parents and peers, cruel snubs from your own household pets, it's all palpable: an all too vividly imaginable world of darkness and despair that could end up as your eternity.

But though you may cringe at intimations of failure as a cockroach panics when he hears the whoosh of an aerosol spray, a monumental lack of success is not necessarily cause for self-extinction. (That prickly possibility—*anything* is possible—will be the subject of a chat below.) Many failures have gone on to lead intermittently happy, quasi-productive lives. We all know about the fictional icons of American *success*, from the Horatio Algers to Ayn Rand's self-absorbed heroes. But the odd man out—the human failure—is not without his own literary niche: Willy Loman, for instance, isn't ordinarily an object of idolatry, but those beaten souls shoved off life's treadmill deserve avatars too.

Just because you're an abject failure in all the meaningful ways does not mean you've no recourse but to spend the rest of your hollow days as a grade school custodian, although many a would-be, never-was captain of industry has found a measure of satisfaction in sprinkling sawdust on the vomit of hysterical schoolchildren.

What constitutes failure exactly? That all depends on you, and your own personal criteria for success. You'll need a good idea of what you *want* before you can authentically feel the sour pangs of lost opportunity. *Webster's* defines failure as "not achieving a particular goal or completing a specific task, to lose," and also as "one who fails, a squinting, squat person who will never merit the friendship of those who are attractive or important."

Success, like Mozart's sonatas, may appear in an infinitude of variations on a theme, but you *always* know when you're hearing Mozart, and experiencing success (which powers of discrimination, incidentally, generally occur in tandem). Failure is stealthier. It creeps up on you, like the silent pumas of legend, and above. Demotions and docks in pay are nearly nonexistent in this Peter Principle age. It's the unusual boss who respects you enough to come out and tell you that you're an embarrassment to the company and, indeed, a pox on the American system of free enterprise. But the pathology of failure is not without general *symptoms.*

THE WARNING SIGNALS
OF FAILURE

1
Ostracism

This symptom is beginning to sound antique and imprecise, like deaths attributed to "old age." Still, at the early stages of prefailure particularly, symptoms may be of a highly diffuse nature, and all you'll sense is a single, great cold shoulder butting against your every desire and utterance. As in domestic intrigues, and terminal illnesses of the more corporeal kind, the victim is often the last to know. Your staff, your secretary, the waitress at the lunch counter, the hooligan who extorts quarters from you on your way to work—they can all somehow smell the noxious by-products of your corroding career, either through a kind of self-preservative sixth sense or by the yellow armband the company issued you last week. Of course they probably won't come right out and tell you—would you if the situation were reversed?—but if the elevator man speaks to you now through a wet handkerchief, and the steno won't sit on your lap unless she sprays Lysol first, there's something seriously amiss. Your secretary may start scooting your lunch in under the door—even the cup of coffee—or you may find her jamming the Whitman sampler you gave her that morning into the paper shredder. Pornographic drawings turn up unaccountably on the shoulder blades of your suit jackets. And if your demise has advanced to a more critical stage, you may have begun receiving anonymous packages of bullets soaked in eels' blood, or a freshly eviscerated raw flounder. Even in this tertiary stage there's no call for a premature dry-dive down the elevator shaft; a promptly applied Ishtar lip tattoo can sometimes ward off the flounder omen, at least, and send your career hurtling back toward the stars.

2
Sores and Cuts That Do Not Heal

Think about it. Have you once met a really successful person covered with shaving nicks, or with unsightly skin lesions of any kind? Dejected antibodies are the first to give up on their compulsion to succeed at all costs and retire to a desultory existence on the cellular dole.

3
Changes in Your Nickname

Just months ago they called you "Tiger" O'Neil, in tones filled with affectionate awe. But at a recent division picnic, two coworkers playing a game of keep-away (from guess who) referred to you as "Scooter," and in the last week or so it's been "What's up, Squeaky?" and "Little late today, eh, Melonhead?" Such a scenario just might be an advance indication of career nose dive. You must take immediate steps to forestall your decline in others' eyes, starting first with a large, colorful lapel badge that says, "HELLO—MY NAME IS GRENDEL."

4
Changes in the Flow
of Office Information

It used to be that all sales memos, say, were always channeled through your office before reaching the president's desk, and your name was near the top of the circulating list for the office copies of *Fortune* and *Dun's Review*. Gradually, the other vice-presidents have begun sending you nothing but abstract doodles and meatloaf recipes. The last periodical you received was a two-month-old *Seventeen* with all the lingerie ads clipped out. They say that *"knowledge is power."* But in our bureaucratic universe, *information is authority,* and the subtle difference is crucial, especially when you're deep into the prefailure phase known as "data deprivation." A fancy computer, installed in your own office for your exclusive use, may be the only realistic solution. A piece of hardware in the one-hundred-thousand-dollar range will do—an I.B.M. 3200, for instance—or maybe just a Maytag 511 if you spring for the extra consoles of superfluous dials and flashing lights.

5
Communiqués from Your Creditors, or from Outer Space Beings

Both possess an alarming (and enviable) ability to find out before you do just how badly your life is going. Bill collectors are not a serious problem for an executive with a secretary willing to run interference and go to prison if necessary. (Two out of the three authors have themselves been through the embarrassment of a repossessed child, and weathered it.) But in the case of the aliens—the ones beaming high-frequency messages directly into your synapses—follow their instructions to the letter. Bishop Pike, for example, was on the precipice of career failure when he wisely heeded the advice of a paper-thin blue creature who carried a jet-propelled attaché and neon aspergillum; within months, Pike was the most famous Protestant clergyman since Martin Luther.

6
Elevators That Seem to Malfunction
Only When You're a Passenger

We know of one officer of a major agribusiness concern who, over a period of months, found himself the victim of increasingly frequent and prolonged elevator stoppages. Less than savvy to the standard omens of imminent failure, he finally spent three weeks stuck between the fifteenth and sixteenth floors. When the half-mad unfortunate was released by a workman preparing to demolish the building, he found that his former employers had confiscated his estate and moved to another country.

7
You Are Passed Over for Promotions
in Favor of Two Illiterate Felons
and Several Inanimate Objects

This, probably, will put a damper on the sturdiest gamesman's enthusiasm. But there's a chance that discouraging snubs like these are only temporary reversals in your Success Schedule. Be patient. Unless you see other, clearer signs of encroaching failure go about your business as if nothing had happened. Deferring to the judgment of a precocious file cabinet may take a little getting used to, but at least you'll be sure of comparative stardom at company softball games. What seems disastrous at first may simply be short-term dislocations resulting from a corporate overeagerness to comply with every conceivable equal opportunity regulation.

These caveats don't concern *you*, you say? Face it: just as a certain percentage of the population must adjust to the prospect of divorce, drug addiction, Down's syndrome, and prefab homes, a portion of you careerists are doing the work of Penelope (but without the happy ending). The statistics prove it. After all, would success be such a neat prize if everyone got a chunk of the fiscal pie? Birds gotta fly, fish gotta swim, and some—maybe you—gotta fail.

It's better to resign yourself to dreams-gone-awry than to wallow in self-pity or rant about the unfairness of life and self-help books that don't really make you an overnight millionaire. Serene acceptance is the key. And there you have a signpost toward one way of coping with failure (or, as we prefer to call it, Significantly Inadequate Success Level). Christ died so that we all might live. And a sense of *Christ-like self-sacrifice,* however illusory, has gotten quite a few ex-rat-racers through the terminal doldrums of failure. We're not saying it's easy. It's not easy at all to smile with a mystical amiability as your former protégé motors by in his new Jensen Interceptor with Miss Utah on one arm and a wristwatch worth considerably more than your home on the other. For the ephemerally inclined—a failed advertising man might do well—this route is a hopeful one. But if Taoist indifference came so damn easily, why were you ever a contender for worldly riches in the first place? This position does have security aplenty: nobody ever replaces a saint with a computer or an eager young Princeton grad.

Fortunately there are several more practical and hard-headed techniques for washing that yellow-gray tincture of failure from your soul. For instance:

Become a Presidential Assassin.
Assuredly this is not a widely available option. There are more than one hundred short, pale loners for every available position, and so you may naturally shrink from competition as rough as that which you bumbled in your prefailure days.

But this is one of the surest ways we know to snatch a *Time* cover story, and it doesn't require four years of college or personal references. All you really need to get started are a passing acquaintance with mail-order gun dealers and with the highway department's parade route coordinator.

Become a Black Person.
Society does not expect blacks to be as successful as whites. Passersby generally express no shock at the sight of a tattered black man reeking of defeat and opportunities denied, slouched in some grotty urban doorway. But if your typical white comptroller, say, were to loiter endlessly on Harlem street corners, people might look askance.

Become a Woman.
Roughly the same logic as above: Successful women are the exception in America. The stigma that adheres to failing females is slight or nonexistent. To forfeit a career-going-nowhere in favor of housewifery may constitute failure objectively, but it's hardly the same as the chronically unsuccessful man working nights down at the country club retrieving stray balls from the water hazards for twelve cents apiece. (Actually, becoming a woman or a black person—assuming you were neither, previously—offers a whole new chance at bona fide success: With the slate wiped clean, you might just be able to play your Affirmative Action hole card and end up supervising those chumps who used to razz you at the water cooler.)

Move to Niger.
In a parched, hungry nation where the per capita income is $138 annually, your failure begins to look not so horrible. They won't think badly of your waffle-weave polyester suits, and a six-foot-tall white man who was an apprentice

credit manager at the W. T. Grant's in Phoenix might seem downright impressive to hunters and gatherers. You might start early preparing for your eventual emigration to Niger: Replace that bowl of Doritos with dried insects, ask your hairstylist to braid dirty twigs into your sideburns, and make constructive use of your coffee breaks by gouging ceremonial scars on your chest.

Forget the Meaning of the Word "Failure."

Nearly every winner in the annals of success has remarked, eventually, that he "doesn't know the *meaning* of the word 'failure.'" You may have not actually succeeded like those platitude-mongering moguls, but you, like them, can become ignorant of words' meanings. Other words whose meanings you should strive not to know are "quit," "lose," "despair," and "bankruptcy." If the chore of willed ignorance seems too hard, then for starters announce to coworkers that you "don't know the meaning of the word 'subreption,'" since you do not.

Ruin the Lives of Successful Men.

Ingenuity is the key here, and the sky's the limit. Detonate a napalm canister in your rich neighbor's doghouse. Send a bevy of obvious call girls to the home of your classmate the company president. Plant heroin poppies in your boss's rose garden and notify the authorities. Mail out thousands of press releases describing how your state's senior U.S. senator, once your childhood buddy, used to masturbate on the American flag after football practice.

Reside in the Land of Narnia.

Depending upon how well you mingle with nymphs and centaurs, this mythical, enchanted place could be a most appealing option. "Success" is a meaningless concept in sunny Narnia, and in this magical world beyond the mists of everyday reality you might find just the oomph you so manifestly lacked working as a free-lance lye merchant. Taxes are low in Narnia, and low-cost condominiums are still in plentiful supply. (Financing is available.)

Dear Success Clinic,

There is nothing so terrible as ignorance in action.
—Johann von Goethe

When we were first teaching our Success Seminars, one question came up more than any other, and it is a question we would like to answer finally, and definitively, right now:

Of course, we're accredited. Don't do anything foolish like call the Better Business Bureau. We're on the level, for God's sake promise you won't phone anybody.

Besides that recurring misunderstanding, however, many other questions arose during the course, and by registered mail afterward. Let us consider some of them here, so that you'll have no need to flood our post office box with thousands of innocent queries and thereby bring a certain postal inspector acquaintance of ours back into the picture.

Dear Success Clinic:
The employees where I work are always either greeting me with broad hellos (what's their insidious game?) or else ig-

noring me completely (these are mainly the people I haven't met yet). It's driving me crazy. Between their phony kindness and their selfish coldness I'm ready to throw in the towel, though by that I don't mean to suggest I'm a washroom attendant, I'm not. I'm an executive on the rise. Don't get the idea I'm everyone's lackey; I am not. Why do people always get the wrong idea about me? I can't see you, so I don't know if you're laughing at me. Don't, please don't. But I'm not begging. Advice?

Our Answer:

Your problem is a common one, and one we sincerely don't mind dealing with for the umpteenth time already. Naturally, in this dog-greet-dog world, none of your coworkers are in the least bit interested in your well-being. I imagine this is particularly true in your case. The act of greeting you is an insult, and the act of *not* greeting you is an insult, though the latter behavior at least smacks only of cruelty and not of hypocrisy.

Still, what do you, as their eventual and inevitable leader, do? Forbearance always makes for good public relations (as if there were any other kind), but in this tooth-and-nail world it's better to make your considerable presence felt. When some sycophant greets you with a cheery "Hello," fix the miscreant with a well-rehearsed steely gaze and counter, "Hello yourself." (Note: At this juncture it is unadvisable to add "big boy" unless you are interested in fisticuffs or ill-defined flirtations. Both waste an executive's time.)

If you want to dumbfound them (as if with awe), answer their twirpy "Good morning" with a cool "It's not over yet" or "*You* may think so." This will upset them to your benefit, especially if their insecurities are in any way commensurate with your own. While you are certainly within your rights to answer any of your cohorts' greetings with "Damn you and your vile good mornings!" it is best to bear in mind that, though you are the deserving one, Fate may temporarily set up decoys by allotting your enemies promotions before yourself.

Dear Success Clinic:
At a recent job interview I of course went on and on about how I loved my prospective employers, how I would gladly recite an oath of allegiance to them daily on rising, and how my family and religion were but shadows of the brilliance the company could shed on my life. The personnel director seemed attentive; then I played a hunch and told him I thought his tie was tasteful and chic. I even offered to buy it. I didn't get the job. Was I wrong to compliment him? Did I go too far?

Our Answer:
Not at all. Your mistake was in not going far enough. Complimenting his tie was an easy and superficial observation; any idiot can dress properly (as we have shown). Flatter your future boss in ways to which he isn't inured. At the interview be quick to praise your interviewer's good physical features. ("I love those long lashes!" "What a small nose for a Sicilian!") Afterwards call repeatedly at his home to demonstrate the sincerity of your gratitude for his time. Write friendly little notes to his wife and each of his children, daily, including photos of yourself. Go into restaurants where he is eating and shush the diners near his table, explaining loudly that your prospective employer is a busy man who requires quiet to think. Tell him you have named your pets after him, and try to dress as much like him as possible. (You can even ask for his cast-off clothes for this purpose.) Adopt his idiosyn-

crasies of speech; imagine his relief to learn that *you* stutter too! Send him coupons you've clipped, or interesting newspaper stories, particularly medical columns relating to illnesses you know afflict him. Write his name thousands of times on one sheet of paper and mail it to him unsigned— though no law says you can't include a return address on the envelope! In short, flatter him with your obsession. He'll feel like a young prince again, and you will reap the happy consequences.

Dear Success Clinic:
At a recent luncheon with the two joint heads of my firm, one of my bosses observed that opera was the ultimate art form. My other boss answered that "Opera is for lily-livered candypants." They both then turned to me. "Well, Simpson, which is it, art or baloney?" they asked. I was petrified. Fortunately, a vice-president at a nearby table had a heart attack at that moment, so attention was distracted from me and the question forgotten in the melee that ensued. If the situation ever arises again, what should I do?

Our Answer:
In such a predicament we advocate suicide.

Dear Success Clinic:
My ex-employer—we're "still friends," understand—has been calling me at home lately, asking if I would "stop by for a little drink sometime." The situation is especially sticky, since my *current* employer (whom I love very much, professionally speaking) was once a wholly owned subsidiary of my former company. Plus the fact that my ex is about to merge with my best friend's marketing division, a merger of which my friend strongly disapproves on religious grounds. What's the correct etiquette given these ingrown

circumstances? Should I visit my ex-employer, but politely refuse that "one little highball"? Or should I invite my boss along to keep everything on the up-and-up? Also, would it be tacky for me to attend the Justice Department hearings on that merger, and on which side of the aisle should I sit if I do attend?

Our Answer:
As we all know too well, a supposedly cordial exchange of pleasantries has, in similar instances, turned into a night of corporate hell for all concerned. It's impossible to predict for certain what old resentments and broken confidences might surface during such an anxiety-fraught reunion. Your wisest course would be to resign your present position, take an assumed name, move to the Hamburg waterfront, and never communicate with either concern again. (And as to that merger ceremony, do you really think you'll be able just to sit back and smile when that big hunk of a marketing division kisses its blushing acquisition?)

Dear Success Clinic:
I am the chief operating officer of a major food-processing concern. Our gross annual revenues, pretax, are now approaching five hundred million dollars. Shortly after eleven this morning, a highly diversified conglomerate made public an offer to purchase controlling stock interest in our company. We don't want them to buy our company. It's ours! The other executives and I have been talking about this darn thing all day long, and I'll be frank with you: we just can't figure out *what* to do, not for the life of us. Help, quick!

Our Answer:
Many corporate boards who should know better consider it "with-it" and "smart" to attempt the takeover of

a smaller company, usually by means of an indiscreet public tender offer. In our book it is *never* proper to buy up all the outstanding shares in a company, at least not without a little warning. A nice, friendly note (on quality vellum!) will do fine. However, since these cloak-and-dagger shenanigans usually resolve themselves within a matter of days or even hours, I imagine your company has already been stolen right out from under you, and you and your management team sacked. Better luck next time!

Dear Success Clinic:
I am suicidal. For years I thought I would grow out of it, but now I must accept the fact that I am not merely distraught with ambition, I am so far beyond the pleasure principle that I can hardly wait for the new pedestrian bridge to open. Does this make me a quitter?

Our Answer:
A suicidal executive is a drain on his family, friends, and colleagues—a kind of social black hole. But this does not mean that if you are suicidal you cannot be successful or powerful. On the contrary, millions of self-hating, demoralized, or just plain bored individuals have bounded like spawning salmon up the flowcharts of corportate power, before reaching—swiftly and decisively—for the final panacea. You can too.

The trick, of course, is in dissembling. You must never let on that you are contemplating the Big S. It is only the sudden, unexpected suicide that can make a mundane life "stoic," or a despicable one "philosophic," and reap your survivors' baffled encomiums.

In conversation with nonsuicidal colleagues (or "straights" as they are called in self-destruction circles), try to cut down on macabre in-jokes spoken inaudibly to yourself. Save meandering stream-of-consciousness monologues for the solo drive home. Weeping should be kept to a minimum. Don't paint Magic Marker stigmata on your palms during working hours.

If you secretly intend to dispatch yourself anyway, exploit this advantage by making momentous decisions with impressive briskness and calm, since you won't be around if hell breaks loose for it later.

Your Boss: What about this Baxter bid for the construction at the new Dallas plant?

You: Go with it.

Your Boss: But they're going to use Styrofoam as support material.

You: I've read all the studies. Go with it.

Dear Success Clinic:
My husband is the environmental compliance officer for a large manufacturer of pesticides. I know he looks the other way when his company dumps large quantities of carcinogenic wastes into our town's water supply. When I confront him on this matter, he pooh-poohs my apprehension and says, "Everybody does it." A couple of years back I told him he ought to put a stop to the practice of releasing invisible clouds of asbestos particles into the workers' changing room, and we nearly separated thanks to that argument. Is it my place to admonish him for contaminating the environment?

Our Answer:
I don't know how many well-intentioned spouses have written with some variation on your concern. I tell all these fretful folks the same thing: *Don't worry your pretty little head about it.* Everyone does do it, and anyway, who says that a

couple of hundred parts-per-million of bug poison's seriously going to hurt anybody? (However, it might be fun to start boiling your own family's tap water for at least two hours before drinking it. Round up the little ones and make a "jungle survival" game out of it.)

Dear Success Clinic:
The problems of short men in business are well-known, but few consider the predicament of tall men in a comparable career. I am such a one (two inches shy of nine feet) and find my dealings with others challenging in the extreme. Beyond a certain height—six foot six, let us say—inch-for-inch increases in respect begin to diminish. Elevators, taxis, airplanes, boardrooms, and restaurants do not become me—the fact that I must stoop and crouch to fit in these places perpetually suggests a servile posture on my part. I am tired of inquiries as to the air up here, and especially since my line is ladies' fine underthings, an aura of unrefinement accompanies my great size. Others fear me without respecting me, and I miss a lot of vital conversation. What do you suggest?

Our Answer:
Since de-elevator shoes are still in the experimental stage, and horizontally striped suits (see "Dressed to Kill") can suggest prison wear, we will have to address your problems otherwise. You could have vertebrae surgically removed, and your leg bones could be shortened, but then your hands would skim along the ground like our friends in the equatorial forests. What you must do is eat. Eat enormous quantities of food, rich food, gloppy, sloppy, heavy food. Become grotesquely fat. Then compensate for your overweight instead of your giantism. Fat, after all, is

much more common. Our book *Diet Your Way to Power* should offer some subsequent pointers.

Dear Success Clinic:
In this informal day and age, is it still considered strictly necessary to send a long, formal tax return to the government every April? It seems like an awful lot of trouble—and positively Victorian in its minutiae. What's your position?

Our Answer:
Although a few of our stuffier friends, prigs for whom tradition and good citizenship die hard, still insist on mailing the I.R.S. the complicated old "Form 1040," the once-charming custom has outlived its usefulness. The Internal Revenue people receive so *many* of these cumbersome "financial R.S.V.P.'s" year after year it's more considerate to the tax men to refrain from adding your forms to the staggering pile. An amiable "Good day" and small honorarium given to your local field agent will more than suffice these days.

Dear Success Clinic:
I don't think I'm so bad. I work at an advertising agency. We do advertisements for people. Okay, I am no crazy man genius like some people, but I don't think I'm so bad. I have a heavy beard shadow and bad skin and shortness but many guys do. I can't seem to get people's attention like the crazy men (geniuses) do. Other people in the agency here where we do advertising for people laugh at me, or it's like they don't even see me or know I'm there, even though I am not so bad. No one notices me, and when I try to write ads I get a blank. How can I get people at the agency (advertising) where I work to do anything I say and I will be like their king.

Our Answer:

First, have many brilliant ideas that no one else has ever had, ideas that, once presented, are obvious and efficient, but completely unprecedented. Be irresistible and charismatic, so even your rivals are flattered by your company.

And use wit in controlling others. It's really very simple: just twist others' words in clever ways to reflect humiliatingly on them, adding insight and flair of your own. They will fear to contradict you if you just see through them and anticipate their every thought. Have what amounts to a sixth sense about all things. That should do it.